CW00557664

The Story of
Green Street Green

MARJORIE FORD &
GEOFFREY RICKARD

THE LONDON BOROUGH

BROMLEY LIBRARIES 2004

FIRST PUBLISHED IN 2004
by
Bromley Libraries
Central Library
High Street
Bromley BR1 1EX
020 8460 9955

ISBN 0 901 002 16 X

Printed by Antony Rowe

CONTENTS

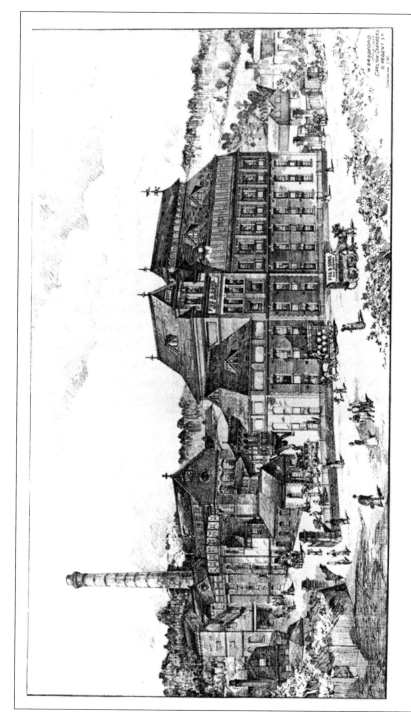

MESSRS. FOX & SONS. OAK BREWERY FARNBOROUGH. KENT.—NEW FERMENTING HOUSE

Oak Brewery in its hey-day about 1900. B.M.

FOREWORD

Village Sign 1953, G.R.

The village of Green Street Green begins in a valley a couple of miles to the south of Orpington, at a point where the roads to Sevenoaks, Orpington and Bromley meet Shire Lane, which leads to Keston and Biggin Hill. At the other end of the village High Street is the road leading to Cudham and Knockholt.

It is an outlying village of Greater London, on the edge of the largest of its boroughs, that of Bromley.

However its history has not been dominated entirely by its larger neighbours Bromley and Orpington. It has its own story to tell.

Whilst most of that story is concentrated round the High Street of the village itself, we have taken as our boundary that of the Parish of St. Mary's Green Street Green.

For almost fifty years the village sign, carved by Mr. Wells and his son in 1952 to celebrate the accession of Queen Elizabeth the second, stood on the Green at the bottom of Farnborough Hill. Its demise in 2001 was the opportunity to have a new village sign designed to commemorate the Queen's Golden Jubilee. It was designed by Stan Mortimer to reflect the history of Green Street Green. We hope that it will occupy its predecessor's place for the next fifty years.

Village Sign 2003, S.M.

INTRODUCTION

The delving into the history of Green Street Green began with our curiosity about the origin of the name World's End. The answer has proved frustratingly elusive, despite the evocative name conjuring fanciful but unsubstantiated possibilities from local legends.

That there was a property called World's End at the Chelsfield end of World's End Lane is well established. It was marked and named on maps from 1798 onwards and existed until 1962 on the present site of Brimstone Close. On a map dated 1769 the property is marked but not named. Geoffrey Copus, who has researched much of Chelsfield's history, including that of World's End, has traced the earliest recorded use of the name to the will of Thomas Mace in 1730. Map makers being somewhat inconsistent in

The Green Street Green end of World's End Lane present day. G.R.

The Chelsfield end of World's End Lane about 1926, B.M.

Brimstone Close present day. G.R.

the past, the name was marked on a map of 1819 in Church Road near the end of the Lane, so perhaps, to the locals, the surrounding area was known as World's End as well as the property itself.

In 1838, the piece of land concerned contained two cottages, the dwellings of farm labourers. The Tithe Terrier lists the property as two 'Cottages and Gardens', one 'Barn and Yard', two 'Orchards' and a 'Field'. William Hills owned all the property and, apart from the two cottages, they were listed as 'Occupied' by him. He was the village postmaster at Chelsfield and owned a shop there as well as other property. World's End does not appear to have been developed or extended, for the occupants named in the 1871 Census (three years after the death of William Hills) were still farm labourers.

In the 1930s World's End Farm was operated as a market garden, including the sale of produce from the orchards. Mr. and Mrs. Hunt, who ran it, moved during World War Two and the farm passed to Mr. Humphries, who carried on a similar business, selling fruit and other produce. Then, in 1962, the farm

The Green Street Green end of World's End Lane early 20th century. B.M.

was demolished and a local builder, Mr. Sanderson, developed the site, creating the present Brimstone Close. Perhaps it was a pity that the Close did not perpetuate the name of the farm but by then the name had officially been applied to the Lane.

So, how did the name originate and why? It is a name used elsewhere in the country, often to denote a boundary point, as also the word 'mark' (as at Keston Mark). In this case it does not appear to have had this function. The relative remoteness of the spot may well be the only reason for its name, despite the legends of Roman soldiers and highwaymen referred to later but there is no firm evidence for any specific origin of the name. For many years World's End Lane was called Chelsfield Road or Chelsfield Lane, in the manner of roads leading towards a particular destination; one wonders how many London Roads there are in the country, for example? The Lane was finally named after a destination nearer than Chelsfield.... or a more distant one, depending on one's philosophical turn of mind.

Sadly, after working on this story over a number of years and waiting even longer for its publication, Geoffrey Rickard will not see the book in print. He died in October 2000 still hoping that it would eventually happen. For his sake, I am delighted that it has at last made its appearance.

Marjorie Ford, August 2003

CHAPTER I

Early Times

Centuries ago the hamlet of Green Street Green developed at what was a convenient stopping place on the route from London to Rye. Now, at the start of the twenty-first century, it is a large village on the edge of Greater London on the busy A21 leading to both the M25 and the Kent Coast. The story of this settlement begins, however, much earlier when the valley, in which Green Street Green lies, sheltered prehistoric animals and primitive people.

The landscape in prehistoric times varied from tropical palms and evergreens to frozen tundra, whilst once the area was submerged by the sea. Fossils, discovered from those times, include shells, sea urchins and a Nipa palm. Archeological finds also reveal that in warm periods deer, hippopotamus, rhinoceros and elephant roamed the valley while in colder times there were reindeer, woolly rhinoceros and mammoth.

In 1862 The Bromley Record printed the story of the 'Discovery of Fossiliferous Remains', describing the 'part of an antediluvian animal', taken

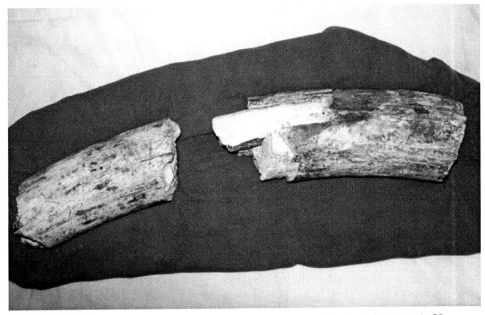

Ivory tusk of a mammoth. G.R.

Tooth of a mammoth. G.R.

from the gravel pit at Green Street Green, at a depth of nearly twenty feet, in a 'very perfect state', though a little damaged. Workmen had dug it up, thrown it on a heap, then had remembered that Sir John Lubbock of High Elms had given rewards for such finds. The account says 'It resembles an elephant's tooth and measures over two feet in length and two or three inches in diameter'. It was identified as the ivory tusk of a mammoth of considerable size and is part of the Avebury Collection at Bromley Museum, Orpington. Another mammoth tusk, found in 1922 *(Bromley Times, December 15th)* is in the British Museum.

Stone Age flint axes found in the gravel deposits of the valley, in Horwood's Pit on the A21, at Old Hill and in Cudham Lane are evidence of the first people to live here but many centuries left few traces of man's development.

Roman Times

Roman habitation is mostly conjecture, from unconfirmed stories of Roman finds such as a mosaic pavement at Pratts Bottom. According to Martin Lee, there was 'a Roman settlement on a hill overlooking Pratts Bottom'. If this were Chelsfield Hill perhaps it was a homesick soldier who first described the spot as 'World's End' but, sadly, this is romantic speculation.

References to Roman roads abound in local lore. Church Road, a continuation of Chelsfield Hill which leads to St. Martin's Church, is said by some local residents to be the oldest road in the area. Others claim the greatest antiquity for Farthing Street, off Shire Lane. Old Hill, the coaching road of later centuries, also has a claim but there is no proof that it was the Romans who first made any of these roads. It is likely that they were already in use as trackways by earlier people.

Old Hill (pre 1914). A.R.

The Grange at Pratts Bottom. G.R.

Church Road remained important for some centuries as it connected Chelsfield Manor with both its Grange at Pratts Bottom and one of the outlying manors, now Norstead Manor Farm.

The Manor of Chelsfield

The Domesday Survey in 1086 showed that Green Street Green was part of the 'Manor of Ciresfil' (Chelsfield), although it did have its own name from quite early days. The first spelling 'grene stroet' is Old English and therefore dates from Anglo-Saxon times when Green Street Green was in the Hundred of Rokesley (Ruxley). In 1292 it had become 'Grenstrete' or 'Grenstretre' but by 1612 it was 'Greene Streete', whilst a map dated 1737 gives the present day spelling.

With so many variations of spelling it is small wonder that the origin of the name is obscure and arguable. Many sources link it with the stories of local Roman roads as the Latin 'strata' (a paved street) having become overgrown, could have acquired the Anglo-Saxon description 'grene'. In the 1855 Post Office Directory a theory is put that it could have been originally 'Greenstead Green', meaning a public green outside the 'stead' or farm of a Farmer Green --or perhaps 'Grinstead Green' from a Farmer Grin. The village did have, until the 1920s, a street with a green at each end and this is the popular explanation of the name nowadays. One will probably never be certain of its origin any more than that of Chelsfield, which has seven recorded spellings.

Even Pratts Bottom, which appears to be fairly obvious (as a hollow belonging to someone named Pratt) has its confusions, being named on a map in 1761 as Locks Bottom and in 1791, when the Porcupine Inn was for sale, being referred to as Spratts Bottom. (Judith Hook - An English Village 1972)

In the centuries following the Domesday Survey there were some national crises, which would undoubtedly have affected the local inhabitants. The Black Death ravaged many parts of the country, striking West Kent very severely and it is estimated that perhaps one third of the population died in 1348 and the following years, although there is no actual record of the deaths locally.

Rebellion and Civil War

In 1450 people living in Green Street Green would certainly have known about Jack Cade's rebellion. His twenty thousand men retreated from

Blackheath through Bromley. They then continued towards Sevenoaks, being joined on the way by some defectors from the King's army. They must have passed through or near Green Street Green and Pratts Bottom, before joining battle with the Royal forces near Sevenoaks. After the defeat and death of Jack Cade grievances were presented to Henry VI on behalf of the people of Kent. Terms were made and pardons given, one Chelsfield name, Johes Jetter de Cheseld, appearing in the list. *(A.T.Waring p.18A)*

Similarly, in 1643, the people of Green Street Green might well have seen military movements between Colonel Browne at Bromley and the Headquarters of the King's supporters at Knole in Sevenoaks. In 1645, some Royalists, in the area of Eynsford, Lullingstone and Chelsfield, rose against the Parliamentarian Sir Percival Hart *(Warlow 1 p.21.)* but there was no large-scale local disturbance.

Parish Registers and Accounts

In 1536, Parish Authorities were instructed to keep records of births, marriages and deaths (the Parish Registers). From these and from the Parish Accounts of Poor Law Relief, dispensed from the Rates collected from local inhabitants, we have a picture of the life of the communities of Green Street

St. Martin's Church, Chelsfield. P.L.

St. Giles' Church, Farnborough. G.R.

Green and Pratts Bottom, for whom the local churches were St. Martin of Tours, Chelsfield and St. Giles, Farnborough.

There were plague epidemics in 1593 and 1603, chiefly in the congested streets of London but local deaths were recorded in Chelsfield and also in the Farnborough Church Registers where, in 1563 in July and August, there were several deaths in some families.

The Farnborough Parish Accounts show that, in January 1717, the assessment made for the 'Releaf of the Poor' was one-shilling (5p) in the pound. This was to be collected by John Wright and Thomas Brook (the overseers) from a list of people assessed at amounts varying from one shilling (5p) to £2.10s. (£2.50), with the poorest people exempted from payment. From the total collected £18.11s.6d. (£18.58), the relief dispensed in 1718 included 'Paid for a yers rent for Thos. Perch £2' and also 'Paid for Bread and Cheas for his wife and family 19s. 11d.' (99p.).

This sort of provision for the labourers and their families is well documented in the Accounts, though the levels of relief were very basic. Farnborough Parish maintained Poor Houses and a cost of £7.13s.9d. (£7.68) is mentioned in the Overseer's accounts in 1807 for thatching them and again in 1815 their repair is mentioned. Chelsfield Parish's Poor Houses were built at Pratts Bottom early in the 17th century, on land taken from the Waste (Common Land). Later, 'Houses of Correction' and then Workhouses were established where the poor were required to work in return for benefits and the Poor Houses were sold to private owners (*Judith Hook*).

By 1756, Chelsfield and Farnborough had formed a 'Union' for the convenient and economical implementation of the Poor Law but the Bromley Union Workhouse at Farnborough, (on the site of the present Farnborough Hospital) was not opened until 1845. The 1834 Poor Law Reform Act had, by then, established such Unions on a statutory basis to be run by Boards of Guardians.

There are many entries in the Farnborough Accounts, which make curious reading in the 21st Century. Whilst it is comparatively easy to guess why, in 1780, 'Mr. Cook's man' should be paid 6d. (3p) for catching pole cats and why, in 1761, someone should be paid 1s.6d. (8p) for 'Stoping ye Rabbett Burrows and taking down ivy from ye Chh Windos', some entries are more obscure.

There are, for instance, a number of references to people being paid, not only for badgers' and foxes' heads (1s. (5p) each) and catching moles in the churchyard (1s.6d. (8p) each) but also for catching the harmless hedgehog, for which the going rate in 1717 appeared to be 4d. (2p) each. In 1754, the rate was still the same, with some intrepid hunter being paid 4s. 4d. (22p) for '13 Hedg Hoggs'. This unusual item, it is believed, reveals the use made of the fat of these creatures for providing light in the church in the dark of winter.

Coaches and Roads

The present day dry valley probably contained in times long ago a tributary of the River Cray or perhaps, some say, its source. That there was a considerable supply of water as recently as 1776, is evidenced by the account of 'the bridge at Green Street Green' needing repair. By the amount of material required, it must have been a large one. (*Blandford p.9*) No site is mentioned, but the pond in front of the Rose and Crown was the most likely place for a bridge, although it is also known that the area near the junction of the A21 with Shire Lane (the old Dump) was swampy ground. There were twelve bridges in all in the area, some existing almost until the end of the 19th Century. (*Blandford*)

The old coaching route avoided the swampy ground, proceeding instead past Farnborough Church, down Church Road, along Shire Lane to Old Hill and thence to the Rose and Crown at the end of Cudham Lane. The use of Old Hill for so many years as part of the London to Hastings road perhaps gave it its reputation as the 'old Roman road'.

As early as 1681 a carrier was plying twice weekly between Tonbridge and Southwark via Green Street Green. Wains, drawn by 8 or 10 horses at 3

mph carried goods. Stagecoaches and the Royal Mail were the only pair horse vehicles. The poorer folk made use of wheeled transport (travelling on the goods carts) long before the horse-riding gentry took to carriages. *(Harper-'The Hastings Road')*
Celia Fiennes said, in her diary of her journey into Kent in 1697, that it was 'but a sad, deep, unpassable road when much rain has fallen' (Jessup p.127). Many roads had to be ploughed up in summer, with the soil left turned in half circles to dry out.

In the reign of Elizabeth the first, a Statute was passed, which ordered that, when heavy goods were transported for a mile on any highway, between 12th October and 1st May, the carrier should also convey a load of cinder, gravel, stone, sand or chalk for the repair of the road on which he travelled. *(Jessup)* The Act was unenforceable and the roads continued to deteriorate.

Later, each parish was responsible for its roads and every male parishioner had to work at repairs for a certain number of days each year or give materials or lend carts or horses in lieu. The parishioners appointed a 'Highway Surveyor' from amongst themselves to oversee this work. The individual concerned seldom had any technical knowledge of the work required. *(Jessup)*

Smugglers

The poor state of the roads might have been to the advantage of one section of the travelling public, the smugglers, for tracking them down and giving chase could not have been easy. They used bridle and field paths, wherever they could, to avoid encounters with the Excise patrols and plied their trade of contraband (mostly liquor) from the Kent and Sussex coasts, up to receiving depots in Bromley (at Walter's Yard) and in Chislehurst Caves. *(Horsburgh p.380)*

'In 1745 a gang of twelve to fourteen such smugglers was surprised on March 12th at Green Street Green by three custom-house officers, with unfortunate results for the officers who were wounded and then robbed' *(Gentleman's Magazine, 1745, p.160), (p.380 Horsburgh).*

The Turnpike Acts

These Acts enabled groups of local landowners to undertake the maintenance of a stretch of road and to charge for its use by erecting tollgates or 'Turnpikes'. Each section of road required its own Act, before the local gentry could institute the Turnpike system and this led to piecemeal development. The Green Street Green, Pratts Bottom stretch was turnpiked in 1748. *(Warlow p.41)* Local landowners contributed for reasons of their own convenience and perhaps a sense of duty but certainly not as a financial investment. It was a difficult system to operate efficiently

THE OLD TOLL-HOUSE, PRATT'S BOTTOM.

Toll House at Pratts Bottom. From Harper, 'The Hastings Road'.

and open to abuse but, with no public authority to supervise road maintenance, it was the only option at the time to keep the roads passable.

Local parishioners were still the road workers. Some men tried to evade their obligations or at best worked grudgingly. In the Farnborough Accounts, there are instances of men avoiding service in the militia, by paying others to go in their stead. For example,'1779 Pd. Mr. Weston for getting one Charles Pullicks to serve as a substitute in ye Militia £4. 4s.' (£4.20) but it was harder to avoid one's obligations on the road. Indeed there is an entry showing that even service in the militia did not absolve a man from his road duty. The Parish Overseers exacted work on the roads in return for Poor Law benefit, an ironical result of which was that the best roads were in places where efficient Overseers had a ready supply of 'Poor' to do the work.

The 1748 Turnpike Act was passed to cover the section of road from 'the well at Farnborough to Riverhill in Sevenoaks' (about 11 miles), which was part of 'the Post Road from London to Tunbridge Wells and to Rye, Sussex'. The local Turnpike gate was at Pratts Bottom, the road continuing up Rushmore Hill and then via Star Hill to Sevenoaks. Prior to the turnpiking, the road was described, in 1748, as 'greatly in decay' by reason of the great and heavy carriages passing through and had become 'very bad in the Winter season', being 'in many places very narrow and incommodious'. *(Warlow - p.41)*

With improved roads and Tunbridge Wells becoming a fashionable venue for wealthy Londoners, 'traffic' must have increased greatly. Stagecoaches were conveying passengers back and forth daily. *(Harper)* One coaching stop was the Rose and Crown, Green Street Green and another the Bull's Head on Rushmore Hill at Pratts Bottom. The hilly nature of the route must have told on the horses, particularly as coaches became larger and heavier, in order to carry more passengers. It became an offence to drive horses too hard up or down Rushmore Hill. *(Martin Lee)* The less arduous route from Farnborough Village via Farnborough Hill and the new road from Pratts Bottom to Dunton Green came many years later. Refreshment for the passengers was almost as necessary as a change of horses, for it cannot have been a very comfortable ride. Hence the dual purpose of the inns as coach stops.

Highway Robbery

A journey from London into the countryside of Kent had another hazard too. Rich pickings were to be had for highwaymen and there are several accounts of robberies, some better authenticated than others. It is known that John Evelyn the diarist had been attacked and robbed in 1652 near Locks Bottom and it is likely that as traffic increased, so did highway robbery. There is a story that the most famous of highwaymen, Dick Turpin, frequented the Bull's Head Inn at Pratts Bottom before being caught horse stealing in 1739 and hanged for his crime. He is reputed to have slept in Pear Tree Cottage, escaping through a tunnel, now bricked up. The Bulls Head is said to have occupied the present site for 400 years. Both the Porcupine Inn, further up the hill and now no longer there, and the Harrow Inn were reputed to be smugglers' haunts. *(Warlow)* Robberies certainly took place around the turn of the eighteenth century. Accounts in the Post Office archives tell of a hold up in 1798 and two in 1801. These were obviously Mail robberies but there may well have been others not recorded. *(Manuscript notes by A.G.Donald, Post Office historian.)*

The most documented hold up was one described in 'The Times' of Wednesday, 3rd October 1798, having taken place on July 31st of that year. A reward was offered of £240 for information leading to the capture of the thief, £40 allowed by the Act of Parliament for the Apprehending of Highwaymen and £200 added as an extra inducement. The robbery had taken place somewhere on the road to Pratts Bottom, when a man on horseback held up the Mail late at night. It is said that the Post Boy in charge tried to deter the armed robber, with the offer of half a guinea (53p) but the highwayman obviously considered that the six bags of mail offered a better deal and he made off with his prize.

Earlier in the day a man on horseback had passed through the turnpike at Pratts Bottom towards Sevenoaks. He returned later asking his way to Croydon and it was considered likely that this was the highwayman. There is no record of an arrest which, given the eyewitness 'description' of a young man of middle size wearing a drab coloured great coat and riding a horse with a white face, is hardly surprising.

James Austin, the perpetrator of a robbery in 1801, was caught and convicted, according to the Post Office file. An additional note records that he was 'hanged in chains'.

The Gibbet

The story of the local gibbet, like so much local history, has many versions. One is that the name World's End reflects the fate of a criminal executed and then displayed as a lesson to other would-be wrongdoers. It is popularly believed, locally, that a gibbet was once sited at the end of the present World's End Lane. If a robbery had taken place, at or near the toll gate at Pratts Bottom, the hill overlooking it would have been a likely place for the gibbet to be placed. In those days a criminal when caught was taken to the county town for trial. If convicted of a capital crime he would be executed there but his body would be taken to be displayed, hanging in chains on a gibbet, at or near the scene of the crime and in as prominent a position as possible, so that other potential miscreants would be deterred. That there was a property named World's End at the junction of the lane with Chelsfield Hill, overlooking Pratts Bottom, is documented as far back as 1730 (Copus 2 p.1) but there is no confirmation of a gibbet at that spot.

There are, however, many references to a gibbet being sited somewhere on Old Hill giving the story at least a ring of truth, despite some contradictory facts. Mr.Fox, who lived at Beechwood in the early 1900s, recounted the story of the gibbet. (Blandford p.13) 'It was fixed on the brow of the hill on the left-hand side of the old coach road, which runs between Lord Avebury's and Mr. Fox's estates. The site was just above the existing old chalk pit, near the gate opening into Mr. Fox's field, from the old road going down into Green Street Green. Mr. Fox states that this gibbet was the last in England to be made use of. The firs near the site were planted to block out the view from their residence.'

Mr. Fox, in telling this story, must have been referring to his family's earlier residence, Oak House, perhaps before he and his family moved to Green Street Green (in 1818), when the house belonged to Samuel Woodhams, a relation by marriage. The use of gibbets ceased in the early years of the nineteenth century. The chalk pit referred to on Old Hill was filled in, in 1909, and the view described no longer exists because of the profusion of trees now growing alongside the by-pass. There were reports that the gibbet and mounting stone were later taken to Chelsfield Hall Farm to be kept but, if this were so, no one now knows their whereabouts. The gibbet would have long since decayed and the mounting stone is probably just another piece of stone somewhere.

Whether this gibbet (assuming its existence) was that of James Austin or of the earlier thief of 1798, we cannot tell but some of the accounts do claim that the criminal was a Mail robber. Another account *(Harper p.54)* cites a mail robbery of 1783, with the gibbeting causing a house to have 'a window bricked up at that time in order to shut out the view of the blackened body of the robber swinging and circling on his gibbet'. The versions vary but the story has caught many writers' imaginations over the years.

It resurfaced briefly in the local press in 1936, when the Beechwood Estate was being built on the land previously occupied by the Fox family home of that name. A workman uncovered some bones from a shallow grave and considerable speculation followed. The story of the gibbet at Old Hill was thought possibly to be connected, with the bones being the skeleton of some criminal, probably a highwayman, who had once hung there in chains. Alternatively it was suggested that the remains were those of a suicide, as it had been customary at one time to give unconsecrated burial, at a crossroads, to those who had committed what was then a crime.

The sequel to the story *(Kentish Times October 2nd 1936)* was perhaps less colourful but even more remarkable, for Sir Arthur Keith FRS examined the bones and pronounced them to be two skeletons, one male and one female, which dated back to a period BC.

CHAPTER 2

Local Administration

During the Nineteenth Century, responsibility for local affairs began to pass from the old Parish system to new Boards and Authorities, which covered larger districts and controlled matters of health, education, law and order etc.

Public Order

The control of the spread of crime, as the population became urbanised, began to be of urgent importance. It was apparent by the year 1829 that a more efficiently organised body was needed to keep order and the Metropolitan Police Force was formed. This did not extend as far as Green Street Green in those early days, however, presumably because at this distance from London the communities were still considered rural. In 1857 the village came under the Kent County Constabulary when the counties began to copy London by replacing inefficient Watches with Police Forces.

County Councils

The Local Government Act of 1888 established elected County Councils from which authority was devolved to Rural District and Parish Councils in respect of education, roads and health and welfare.

B.R.D.C. to O.U.D.C.

Local government of the area at this time was administered by the Bromley Rural District Council, which delegated some functions to the Parish Councils, twelve in all. Two of these, Chelsfield and Farnborough, covered Green Street Green. The reorganisation of local boundaries, effected by the 1929 Local Government Act, caused the Bromley R.D.C. to be wound up and in 1934 the Orpington Urban District Council was established to cover the parishes of Chelsfield and Farnborough, as well as Downe, Cudham, Knockholt, St. Mary Cray and Orpington itself. It was one of the largest U.D.C.s in the country. It had representation on the Kent County Council of two members and was also represented on the West Kent Main Sewerage

Board and the West Kent Hospital Board. The Metropolitan Police covered the northern part of the Urban District but the southern villages were still covered by the Kent County Police.

Bromley - The London Borough

In 1965 the Greater London Council came into being and its largest borough was the London Borough of Bromley. Orpington was swallowed up and with it the outlying villages, including Green Street Green and Pratts Bottom. At the time there is no doubt that many people resented the change and felt that Orpington would become a poor relation of the now more important Bromley, an opinion still held by some today. People in the villages probably felt even more on the fringe of this large borough. Locally it was not popular but became accepted as inevitable. Knockholt fought successfully to be excluded from the takeover. Local Residents Associations are important in keeping village issues aired and opinions heard, the Green Street Green Association being an efficient watchdog in this respect, keeping the last vestiges of independence.

Public Health

As communities grew in size, there was a need for better welfare organisation. Boards of Guardians took over the care of the poor from the Parishes after the 1834 Poor Law Act. Public health also became a matter needing public action in the later years of the nineteenth Century.

The water supply and drainage of the whole area came under review in the 1870s, as a potential health hazard because of repeated cases of cholera, typhoid and a particularly bad outbreak of scarlet fever. In 1854 there had been cases of Asiatic Cholera and two Chelsfield women had died. The change began as the unhealthy cess pool system was replaced by properly laid sewerage, by underground pipes installed by the West Kent Sewerage Board. How slow this was to become general in Green Street Green is instanced by the existence of septic tanks behind some of the old houses, up to as recently as the 1970s.

Drinking water was drawn from the three wells in Green Street Green until almost the end of the nineteenth century. One belonged to the brewery, one was up World's End Lane near the present vicarage and the third was outside the house known as 'Wellhurst', opposite the old school in the High Street. They were deep wells, the brewery well being below the chalk level over a hundred feet down. It still existed, below the cellars, when first Telcon Plastics and then Medway Packaging occupied the site. The water from this well was said to be exceptionally pure. Water from the well opposite the school had been sold in the mid - nineteenth century at a 1/2d. per pail (about 0.2p), the locals queuing up each morning to fix their buckets to the hook, lower the rope and obtain their halfpennyworth. Most houses had underground rain water cisterns, from which the water for domestic use was either pumped or drawn up in pails until, in 1877, the West Kent Water Company began to supply the residents of the Farnborough area with piped water. It was to be a hundred years before some of the houses acquired bathrooms and indoor sanitation, although water mains had been laid in 1889.

Medical attention for the poor had barely existed in the past, although various remedies had been dispensed to the sick of the Parish from the Poor Law rate. Seldom, however, is there a mention of a doctor, so much of the treatment was of the 'Old Wives' variety. The first Medical Officer for the 'Poor of the Parish' (Farnborough) was appointed in 1823 at an annual salary of £18. 18s. (£18.90). In 1880, the nearest doctors were four miles away at Keston or six miles distant at Riverhead but by 1890 there was a doctor in Orpington and the Cray Valley Hospital in Sandy Lane was founded.

Orpington Hospital

It took a world war to bring a hospital to Orpington. It was built for the military in 1915 and 1916 and the Province of Ontario in Canada, which levied a small charge on all its residents to help the war effort, financed it. An extension was built in 1917, making a total of 2000 beds. Soldiers from all over the Commonwealth (but mostly Canadians) were brought from the battlefields and those who died in the hospital were buried in 'Canadian Corner' in the churchyard of All Saints Church in Orpington. The wounded were brought by rail from the coast and the trains were halted on the embankment alongside the hospital, so that the wounded could be transferred directly, out of public sight.

After the war the hospital was sold to the British Government for £80,000 and the Ministry of Pensions took it over for ex-service men. During the Second World War Orpington Hospital was again used by the Military. In the inter war years it had been an Air Force training establishment and in the 1930s was used by Kent County Council. Early in the war a large contingent was evacuated from Guys Hospital and a new block by the embankment was built to accommodate the numbers needing treatment. Many casualties were received especially from the evacuation of Dunkirk.

After the war it became a general hospital and in 1953 a nurses' teaching school was set up. In 1979 most of the original 1916 huts were demolished to make way for the present Canada Wing. This was planned as Phase 1 of

Ontario Military Hospital, Orpington 1916. J.B.

A ward at Christmas 1917. J.B.

a new general hospital, which sadly never became a reality. Farnborough was the choice for the new hospital and much of the Orpington site was sold for a large housing estate, with the Canada wing being kept for some rehabilitation wards and clinics. The League of Friends was formed in 1951 and has continued its supportive work for Orpington Hospital up to the present day, with its active campaign for the new Hydrotherapy Pool.

A village Doctor and Nurse

There was a doctor in Green Street Green by the 1920s, when Dr. Benyon had his surgery at 'Middle House', the round-ended building at the south end of the High Street.

Middle House, Green Street Green (early 20th century). A.R.

The idea of employing a District Nurse had been discussed by the Chelsfield Parish Council before the end of the nineteenth century and in 1900 Nurse Hardy was appointed, her salary coming from the fund set up for the purpose. The annual subscription paid by the local residents was a minimum of 2s.6d. (12 1/2p), payable as a lump sum or in instalments. By 1917 it was felt necessary to raise Nurse Hardy's salary to £100 per year but, despite fund-raising efforts, the District Nurse Fund was no longer self-supporting and the post could not be maintained.

In 1922 requests to re-instate it led to the suggestion that a local nurse in each hamlet could undertake the work and collect her own fees. The idea was dropped, whether as unnecessary or unworkable is not clear. 1948 and a National Health Service were then still far off. In the 1980s the village gained the valuable amenities of surgeries for doctors and dentists and a much-needed chemists in Brittenden Parade. By the year 2000, there was an additional doctors' surgery, on the corner of Laxey Road, to cope with the increase in population.

CHAPTER 3

Expansion of the Village

The village in the 1870s. A.R.

From studying old maps and photographs, we get an idea of the building that went on in the final quarter of the nineteenth century and the consequent growth in population. A map of 1871 shows only scattered properties. The Queen's Head public house is on the corner of World's End Lane with a row of cottages or shops on the other corner. The Lane is undeveloped, apart from four cottages at Simons Haw (the present vicarage site) and some properties at the Chelsfield end of the Lane, one of which is identified as World's End. We can see Oak Brewery, Green Farm, Lower Green Farm and also Chelsfield Hall Farm, but not its cottages, built a little later in World's End Lane. The old School in the High Street is marked, as are the houses nearby (built in 1867). The Larches and the Rose and Crown are there and houses at the foot of Old Hill, one of which was Laundry Cottage with its long ironing room, where the Fox family laundry was done.

A photograph shows just how undeveloped the area was a few years later, even after some additional building in the High Street. The map of 1896

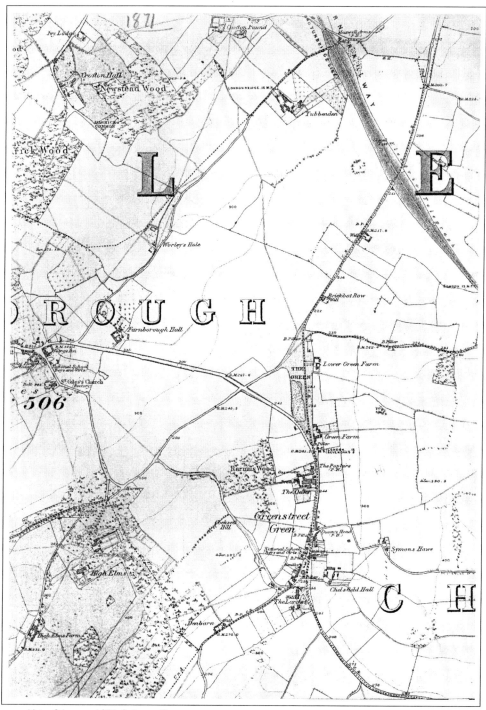

Map of the area 1871. Ordnance Survey.

records that more building had taken place at the foot of Old Hill, whilst in World's End Lane there were houses on the corner of the present Kingsley Road, a row of cottages below Ash Road and a few houses in Ash and Elm Roads. In the High Street, on the site of the Social Club, which was in existence until as recently as 2001, was a building marked 'Mission Room',

Cottages (late 19th century). P.L.

built by the Brewery owners for their employees. The coachman's house and stable (now the Community Centre) is marked next to Fox's Brewery, where there was considerable employment as the business expanded and flourished. This brought the need for shops and encouraged other small ventures like that of Mr. Twist, who had set up a soap business, in the row of cottages at the bottom of World's End Lane. He sold his tablets of soap for sixpence each, advertising its 'floating' property as an enticement to buy.

An eyewitness description of Green Street Green in 1906 *(Harper p.53)* describes the village somewhat unflatteringly saying 'we cannot altogether avoid the ugly, which appears very large and brutal, in the Oak Brewery. I am told it is a very famous brewing firm but one willingly forgets their name and only knows that their buildings are ugly and sooty and look dry and make one feel thirsty. Perhaps there is more in that than meets the eye.'

The existence of a large industrial building was obviously a shock to the aesthetic senses but the blow is softened a little by the additional information that 'Green Street Green really has a green ' and 'it is rather a large and not unbeautiful specimen.'

The Farrants were a landowning family in the area for a couple of hundred years at least. There is a monument to Thomas Farrant dated 1680 in Cudham Church and a century later, in 1784, Norsted Manor was alienated to the family. They owned all the land later known as Glentrammon Park, which estate went up for sale in 1887. It stretched from the High Street up to Waring Close and from Green Farm Close and Highfield Avenue to World's End Lane and the 'Tree Roads'. This included Simon's Haw and the piece of land on which Farrant Close now stands. This sale was what brought about the first large-scale housing development in Green Street Green.

Into the twentieth century

A photograph taken during the first decade of the twentieth century shows a change in the appearance of the village, with building in progress in Kingsley Road. Maps, too, show the development of roads and property.

The village inthe early 20th century. A.R.

By 1909, Glentrammon, (formerly New Road) Laxey, Lezayre, Kingsley and Dowlerville roads were all named, as were all five 'Tree Roads', Ash, Elm, Oak, Beech and Holly. These maps show plots sold and houses built, the agent for the 'Tree Roads' having been a Mr. James Dowler, a sand, ballast and chalk merchant, after whom Dowlerville Road was named. Mr. Dowler, so the story goes, grew enormous quantities of sweet peas and fruit, which he

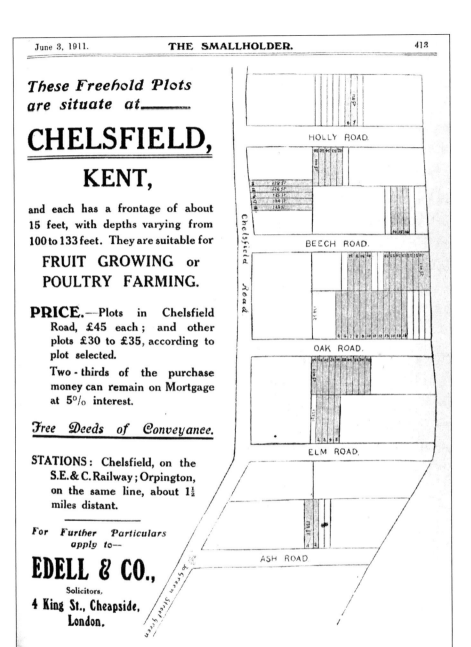

These Freehold Plots are situate at_____

CHELSFIELD,

KENT,

and each has a frontage of about 15 feet, with depths varying from 100 to 133 feet. They are suitable for

FRUIT GROWING or POULTRY FARMING.

PRICE.—Plots in Chelsfield Road, £45 each; and other plots £30 to £35, according to plot selected.

Two-thirds of the purchase money can remain on Mortgage at 5% interest.

Free Deeds of Conveyance.

STATIONS: Chelsfield, on the S.E. & C. Railway; Orpington, on the same line, about 1½ miles distant.

For Further Particulars apply to—

EDELL & CO.,

Solicitors,

4 King St., Cheapside, London.

Advertisement from 'The Smallholder' 1911

presented to prospective buyers to ensure their interest in purchasing a house. This area, known to the locals as 'Burton's plots', had also had, as an attraction for visitors, a large cave somewhere between Elm and Oak Roads facing Hillcrest Nursery, which was on the opposite side of World's End Lane. This cave was perhaps left by the extraction of chalk, some time previously. The roads Glentrammon, Laxey and Lezayre were named by William Crafter, their builder, as a happy reminder of a family holiday spent in the Isle of Man.

In 1912 the small row of shops at the bottom of Lezayre Road was built and named 'The Broadway', the description 'High Street' seeming to have come much later.

The 'Broadway' about 1912. B.M.

As for World's End Lane, although it had, by 1909, a number of properties it was not named on the Kent Survey map. For some reason this lack of an official name was to continue for many years, with people referring to it variously as Chelsfield Lane, Chelsfield Road or World's End Lane or Road in a seemingly random manner. A Post Office at the corner of Ash Road, which had been there since at least 1890 had, in the early 1900s, the confusing post mark of Chelsfield Lane Post Office, Green Street Green, Chislehurst because Chelsfield mail was then handled by Chislehurst. In 1911, on a map on the Bill of Sale of Edell & Co., the name Chelsfield Road is given for the same stretch of road. There must have been much confusion over addresses, particularly as the houses had only names not numbers, the numbering being done only as recently as the 1970s.

The 'Broadway' present day. G.R.

Post World War I developments

The council houses in the High Street were built in the 1920s and Glentrammon Road and Vine Road were extended. Despite the expansion of the village it became a quieter place when, in 1927, Farnborough Way cut across Farnborough Hill and Shire Lane to make a by-pass for both Farnborough and Green Street Green. Mrs. Dora Saint (Miss Read, author of the Thrush Green books), who lived on Chelsfield Hill at the end of Worlds End Lane, held a similar opinion of the village in the 1920s, to that quoted from A. C, Harper earlier. She described it in a letter to us as being 'rather a scruffy place along the main London to Hastings road' when she was small but added that it improved a lot as it began to join up with Farnborough.

From 1920, Homesteads Ltd. (Est. 1903) began housing development in this area, one of four sites around the outer edges of London. The building took place over a considerable part of Green Street Green, from Julian Road up both sides of World's End Lane almost to its end and also on Sevenoaks Road, from Chelsfield Hill to The Hillside. New roads, Homestead, Oxenden Wood, The Meadows, The Woodlands and The Meadway were developed. Photographs were available to prospective buyers of the different houses and bungalows, which were to be built on the plots. In a booklet for 1934 prices for plots, which ranged from about a quarter of an acre to one acre, averaged from £80 to £260. In that year the local manager, Mr. P. H. C. Curtis, lived at

BEECHWOOD ESTATE

Farnborough Hill, Orpington, Kent.

FREEHOLD

Detached Houses - £695.

Accommodation:
Lounge, 13 ft. by 11 ft.
Dining Room, 11 ft. 6 in. by 11 ft.
Partly Tiled Kitchen
Tiled Bathroom and W.C.

1st Bedroom, 13 ft. by 11 ft.
2nd Bedroom, 10 ft. by 11 ft.
3rd Bedroom, 10 ft. 6 in. by 7 ft. 3 in.
Ample space for Garage

Ideal Boiler — Gas Fires in Bedrooms

Only the best Workmanship and Materials used in the construction

CAVITY WALLS   Furnished Show House Open to Inspection at all times.

COLEMAN CONSTRUCTION Co., Ltd.

ESTATE OFFICE ON SITE.

Semi-Detached Houses £625.

Accommodation:
Lounge, 19 ft. 2 in. by 10 ft. 3 in.
Dining Room, 10 ft. by 9 ft. 3 in.
Partly Tiled Kitchenette

1st Bedroom, 12 ft. by 10 ft. 3 in.
2nd Bedroom, 11 ft. 5 in. by 9 ft. 3 in.
3rd Bedroom, 10 ft. 3 in. by 7 ft. 6 in.
Tiled Bathroom and W.C.

Electricity   -   Main Drainage.

NO Road Charges. Legal Fees. Survey Charges.

These Houses and inspection by Builders and Surveyors is invited   GRAVEL SOIL.

95% of the purchase money can remain on mortgage if required

A. J. BOTTING & Co., Surveyors,

106, JERMYN STREET, S.W.1.   WHITEHALL 0035

Advertisement from The Orpington Guide, 1935.

Julian Brimstone on Church Road and he remained resident there until the 1950s. World's End Farm was not included in the Homesteads plan at that time, the site being developed much later.

Bromley is described in 1901 as having 'streets of houses fitted with electric light, hot and cold water supply and drained in accordance with the latest improvements' *(Harper p.36)*. It was much later that some of these amenities reached Green Street Green. It was, in fact, the end of the nineteenth century before oil lamps and candles began to be replaced by gaslight, supplied by St. Mary Cray Gas Company. Electricity was a twentieth century improvement, installed only as recently as about 1980, in some of the older houses in Green Street Green.

Not until 1935 did the Orpington Journal report, in its 'Chelsfield Chat' column on November 9th, that 'World's End Lane has got its gas lamps and the entire length of it from The Queens Head to Church Road is now illuminated'. It added hopefully 'A couple of lamps on Chelsfield Hill would be useful'.

The Beechwood Estate present day. G.R.

There was still growth in the village in the 1930s despite the hard times. The Beechwood Estate was built in 1935 and included in the Parish of Green Street Green, although cut off from the village by Farnborough Way. Semi-detached houses were sold for £625 and detached ones for £695, all with three bedrooms, and mortgages of 95% were available. The builders were Coleman Construction Company Ltd. and purchase was made more

Windsor Drive present day. (Library P10/11)

tempting by the fact that there were no road charges, no legal fees and no survey charges.

The Green Belt

After WW2, development went on in Warren Road and Cloonmore Avenue and the Windsor Drive estate was built in the 1950s on the cornfields leading up to Chelsfield Station. Later, in the 1960s, the Highfield estate and then the roads off Glentrammon Road were built. These developments apart, the growth of the village continued piecemeal as before, with small areas or individual plots being built on as land was sold.

Fortunately the Town and Country Planning Act of 1947 prevented what could have been an urban sprawl coming through and beyond Green Street Green, by confirming the pre-war commitment to a Green Belt around London. Local authorities had, since 1938, been empowered to purchase land, which might otherwise be acquired by property developers. The A21 at Green Street Green was declared the limit of the Orpington boundary for development. Requests for building permission beyond the limit have since that time always been refused. Similarly the Common land at the other end of the village has been jealously guarded from potential development, as it had been in earlier times. *(Copus p.4)*

Further expansion

Expansion continued within the village, as old property was demolished or parcels of land were sold off from large gardens. The stretch of land left vacant for the proposed London Orbital Road was finally sold for housing.

There may still be odd plots on which to build in Green Street Green but, with the building of Moat Close (off Dowlerville Road) in the 1980s and the Oaks Estate on the Brewery site and Flint Close behind the old Social Club, the village seemed to be complete. However, the Parish has again grown considerably, since the house building on the Orpington Hospital site. The demise of the Social Club and the possibility of the demolition of two houses next to the old school could bring further housing development. No longer the hamlet it once was, Green Street Green does still manage to retain its village identity.

CHAPTER 4

Village Life

Green Street Green started as a farming hamlet and remained as such until the advent of Fox's Brewery in the nineteenth century.

Chelsfield Hall Farm

Chelsfield Hall Farm, often referred to as Green Street Green Farm, near the A21 roundabout at the southern end of the High Street has existed since at least 1612, when it was mentioned in the Court Rolls of Chelsfield, as the property of Edward Ferby the Sheriff of Kent. Another opinion dates it further back to 1542. Some of the present building is known to be seventeenth century or earlier, with the southwest wing dating from the eighteenth century.

There are several stories associated with the farm. At one time a hole, thought to be a hiding place for silverware, was discovered in the dining

Chelsfield Hall Farm present day. (Library 011/28)

room behind a fireplace. Its use as such, and the whereabouts of the possible contents, is unconfirmed.

A building (now demolished), which used to adjoin the house, was allegedly built on foundations of whalebone. The building was said to have stood three or four feet above ground. Samples of bone, sent to the Natural History Museum, had been identified as those of the blue whale.

Another story (already mentioned) places the last remains of the Old Hill gibbet at Chelsfield Hall Farm but sadly, no one now has any knowledge of their having been there.

Green Farm

At the bottom of Glentrammon Road (known in 1897 as New Road) Green Farm stood for a couple of centuries on the corner overlooking the start of Farnborough Hill. At this end of the High Street there is no longer a farm, as there is at the other end but there the Green has gone, whilst here the Green has been preserved as Common Land.

Green Farm about 1900. A.R.

Lime Tree Cottage

It is therefore strange to see a house, Lime Tree Cottage, standing on what is, or was, undoubtedly part of the Green next to old Warren Road It was recorded in the Chelsfield Court Rolls in 1814 that a grant had been made by the Lord of the Manor of Chelsfield, George Morland, to Edward Bassett of a piece of Waste at Green Street Green, the term 'Waste' meaning a piece of Common land. Although the Lord of the Manor was not entitled to dispose of Common land in this way and his right was queried, no further action was taken and the grant stood. It is recorded that Bassett had built on the land and a Quit rent of fifteen shillings (75p) was agreed. The tenancy changed hands from Edward Bassett to John Stevens (or Stephens) and then to George Whale. *(Copus p.5)*

Lime Tree Cottage present day. G.R.

In 1860 the 'Messuage, garden and appurtenances lately Waste' were freed forever by payment of twenty-one pounds to extinguish the Quit rent owed to the Lord of the Manor. All feudal obligations were revoked by this agreement and the cottage has remained in its unique isolation on the edge of the Green ever since. The original building has been extended but its appearance has been maintained and it still has an old-world charm.

In 1912 Mrs. Valentine Moon bought the cottage from Mr. Osgood, a prominent local resident, and it became known until the 1960s as Mrs. Moon's Tea-Rooms. Generations of local children bought their sweets there. Mrs. Moon's grandson (with, until relatively recently, his mother) still lives in the cottage, which has been best known for the delight it has given, over the years, to passers-by at Christmas. Its transformation by coloured lights into a veritable fairy-tale cottage, added to the attraction of the 'not unbeautiful' Green.

Captain Swing

In this farming community in the early decades of the nineteenth century crimes were predominantly rural in character. In 1830 there were disturbances in many parts of England as agricultural labourers were enduring great poverty, hunger and the threat to their jobs of new farm machinery. In some counties there was considerable violence against people and property and many perpetrators were caught and tried. A few were hanged but most were imprisoned or transported to Australia.

The leader of these disturbances was a 'Captain Swing' who, despite being a fictional invention, posted warning notices on farm gates and wrote threatening letters, as reported in The Times of October 2nd 1830.

Whilst there are no accounts of serious violence against people in this area, it is known that by the end of September 1830 there had been some thirty or so instances of arson round Bromley, Orpington and Sevenoaks. Barns and hay ricks were the targets and it is said that local people not only stood and watched the fires burn but they actually hindered the firemen and volunteers in their efforts to put out the flames.

At one fire in the Orpington area 'the labourers stood by a burning barn and said "Damn it, let it burn. I wish it was the house; we can warm ourselves now; we only want some potatoes; there is a nice fire to cook them by' (Wright p.146). Inhabitants of Green Street Green may or may not have been numbered among the arsonists but, most local people being farm labourers, one can imagine that their sympathies were with 'Captain Swing'. The campaign was short lived, although the misery went on for the agricultural poor with further efforts to improve their lot meeting with harsh punishment, as at Tolpuddle in 1834.

Agriculture in the later 19th century

Farming, although no longer the main occupation of the local men folk was still important but was taking a new direction. Fruit farms, from Plumstead and Erith to Cudham and Knockholt and from Farningham to Farnborough covered a wide area of Northwest Kent, by the late nineteenth century. (Harvey p.222)

The acreage in the neighbourhood of the Crays and near Dartford, Orpington, Chelsfield and Farnborough consisted mainly of raspberries, currants and gooseberries (SouthEastern Gazette 11.9.82) but there were also over 2,000 acres of strawberries. In the description of Fox and Sons Brewery (Barnard p.4) the drive from Orpington Station is described as 'past acres of strawberry fields.' One can imagine the summer air heavy with the sweet smell from such acreage. Even the allotment holders seem to have been fruit growers. A Chelsfield Church Magazine for 1895 expresses concern for the local allotment holders' fruit growing and harvesting and the effect of the weather and insects on the crops. To control pests the suggestion was made that growers 'will never find a method at once so effectual and so cheap as to have a fair stock of small birds.' No advice was given about the practicalities of this method of pest control!

As the nineteenth century ended, hop fields, corn fields, strawberry and raspberry fields covered much of the land surrounding the village and many villagers still worked on the land. There were cornfields up towards Chelsfield, as well as on either side of the main street. In the autumn the corn was threshed by machinery and the straw was sold, after which the villagers were allowed to glean the fields. They would take their gleanings along to Hodsoll's water mill at Cray Avenue, where it would be ground while they waited. They would return with sometimes as much as half a sackful of flour - a bonus for a poor farm worker's family in hard times. Proximity to London markets encouraged the dominance of fruit growing in this locality until later in the twentieth century when land began to be lost to suburban development and faster road and rail transport made trips to market from other areas more competitive.

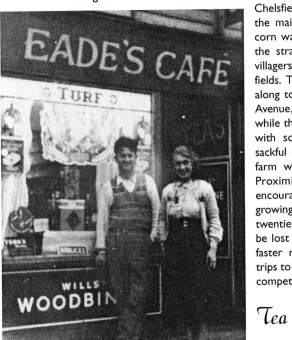

Eade's Café in the 1930s. B.M.

Tea Rooms

Whilst farming and brewing were indeed the mainstays of the village, by

Wellhurst in the early 20th century, the site is soon to be redeveloped. P.L.

The Bombay Brasserie present day. G.R.

the early twentieth century its position as a convenient stopping place on the Hastings Road brought forth a proliferation of refreshment places.

One such was in the 'Middle' or 'Round' House at the south end of the High Street, later known as Winnie Eade's. In 1905 when Green Street Green had five tearooms, that one had the distinction of being listed in Strong's Directory as a 'Coffee-House'. Opposite there was also Wellhurst, its name presumably derived from the well which used to be nearby. It is listed in the Appraisal Area Report for Chelsfield and Goddington, compiled by Bromley Borough in 1981, as an L-shaped building of the eighteenth century with nineteenth century additions. It was at one time used as a residence for senior employees from Oak Brewery but in the early years of the 20th century it was Ye Olde English Tea House. The lawns in front made a pleasant spot for a summer afternoon tea party. Several dwellings now occupy some of the land where the 'Sixpenny Teas' (2$\frac{1}{2}$p) were served.

Winnie Eade's Coffee-House became Kath's Cafe in the 1950s but by then all the other tea-rooms had gone, including the one at the bottom of Old Hill in Mrs. Naylor's General Store, there in the late 1920s. In recent years the fashion for more exotic food has produced 'The Bombay Brasserie' in the old Coffee House and the village now boasts other Indian, Chinese and Turkish cuisine but no 'Teas'!

The Boer War

Various European wars, trouble with the Scots and Irish and rebellion in the American colonies were all major events in British history in the eighteenth and nineteenth centuries. No direct evidence of the involvement of any local people in such events exists until the Boer War when the second battalion of the Royal West Kent Regiment went out to South Africa to fight and people at home started a 'Comforts Fund' for the troops. In June 1900 Mrs. Grove, wife of Lieutenant-Colonel Grove, thanked all those who had contributed to the Cardigan Fund which had sent out five cases of warm clothing to the soldiers. By then one local man had lost his life in South Africa. Sergeant Frederick Walter Shells of the Larches was killed on May 27th 1900, fighting with the Middlesex Yeomanry. The brass lectern in Farnborough Church is dedicated to his memory.

World War I

With so many of the country's men involved in the armed services it was essential for those left in civilian life to assume duties other than their normal occupations. One impressive example of this was the 4-man motorcycle fire brigade used in 1917 to fight fires in the Orpington District.

Based at Green Street Green it was manned by four local traders, Mr. Frank Whittaker, a local cyclemaker (the driver), the butcher, Mr. Davey, the grocer, Mr. Skilton and a builder, Mr.Baugh. All were volunteers and the motor cycle combination was always ready to proceed promptly to the scene of any local fire.

Whilst life in Green Street Green might have been exciting for the fire brigade volunteers, this small Kentish village must have been a rather unexciting place for others, as is revealed by a postcard sent by one homesick soldier, billeted in the disused brewery. It is dated 25th October 1917 and is as follows...

World War I fire engine. B.N.

'My Dear Jessie, I have been looking out for a photo of our barracks, just to get you an idea of what the place looks like. I got this one in Farnborough, a night or so ago. It is a fairly good one and gives you a decent view from the front. There are two gates into the place, one on either side of the building, the one on the right for non-commissioned ranks and the left one for officers only. Just to the rear of the chimney marked with a cross, which you are unable to see, is where our club is situated. We are very comfortable in it and have a nice fire at nights making it quite homely. Where you see the crosses, in the front view below the ground are our company quarters, which are nothing to talk about. The field in front leads up to our training ground, to the bayonet course. We are surrounded in lovely scenery but the place is terribly quiet, so you can imagine going to bed early 8.30 every evening I have never had so much bed for months. Orpington is quite a scattered village, houses in about fifties here and there extend for a good distance either way. We are not having bad weather fairly cold of course but one thing it is fresh air that we do get. If we go out at night we generally are back by 7.30 feeling quite satisfied for the evening......Stanley ..'. (This card, presumably posted in an envelope, for it carries no address or stamp, is in the collection of Bob Turner 1988).

The Brewery as a barracks in W.W.I.P.L.

One local resident having an eventful time during the war, was Miss K. Stacey of Green Street Green. Her name featured in the local press, when it was reported that she was the first trained nurse to go abroad to tend the forces in the 1914/1918 war. She served in Malta and Salonika, was mentioned in dispatches for her bravery and work, and was awarded the Red Cross Medal 2nd Class and the French Government's Medal of Honour. In the last few decades of the nineteenth century the name Stacey occurred regularly in the Chelsfield Church Registers. In 1902 James Stacey had a coal merchant's business in Green Street Green and by 1930 it was William Stacey of Sterne Cottages who was running it. There are still some families named Stacey living in and around the village.

Life in the 1920s and 1930s

Green Street Green had become quite a flourishing community, to judge from the number of newly formed local societies. A Literary and Social Society was formed in 1924, the Horticultural Society in 1925, the Camera Club in 1925, the Girl Guide Company in 1928 and the Dramatic Society (the Greenfield Players) in 1928. There must have been considerable community spirit in the village as these groups added to the existing church activities, although we have no membership records to indicate the level of support.

Making a film in the village would cause a stir even in our media-conscious days, so one can imagine the excitement in 1922, when filming took place somewhere near Middle House, (the Round House). It was, of course, a silent film and some of the local people were used as 'extras'. They were paid half a crown (25p), a rich reward in those days for the chance to take part in such an exciting event. The film was originally called 'The Price of Silence' but its title was changed to 'Shifting Sands'. It was an adventure film set in Tripoli, so the choice of Green Street Green as a location was, to say the least, surprising. It was a six-reel film directed by the American Director, Fred Leroy Granville. Sadly, according to the National Film Theatre, no copy has survived.

In 1925 'Arkies' (formerly The Elms, one of the houses used for important Brewery employees), then a hotel-cum-lodging house next to the school in

Advertisement from 'The Orpington Journal' 1925.

the High Street, became a tennis centre. Three public hard courts were open from 6 a.m. for 'Town Workers' (today's commuters) to play before work. Refreshments were available, or, for the more sophisticated, there was the fully licensed 'Old Pantile Club' with social amenities. The venture failed after the Farnborough by-pass separated the courts, (roughly where the Rose and Crown car park is now) from the hotel. Later, In the 1930s, the original Royal Oak moved into 'Arkies' from the Round House.

In the 1920's' two residents of Green Street Green were featured in both the local and national press, when they celebrated the fact that they were the oldest married couple in the country. John and Sophie Taylor were both born in 1824. John celebrated his 102nd birthday in April 1926 and Sophie in August. They were married sixty-six years earlier, having met in 1855. By the time the articles were written, Sophie was bedridden, living in an upstairs bedroom in their son's house. John was not strong enough to climb the stairs, so they no longer saw each other but communicated by messages conveyed by their son. Sophie lived only another year until she was aged 103 but John did not die until 1929 when he was 105. Their story was featured in The Daily Chronicle of April 14th 1924.

Messrs. Penfold and Brodie, who ran a private hire coach company, offered their services in 1926 during the General Strike and provided milk suppliers and the General Post Office with vehicles and drivers. Mr. Brodie subsequently set up a separate business based at Farnborough Hill. In 1936 Mr. Penfold also ran a lending library, charging 2d. (1/2p) per book per week and advertising 'New titles weekly at the Motor Coach Depot'. Business was restricted during the war but coach trips were resumed after 1945. The ownership of the site changed to Lewis' Coaches, until the development by Waitrose in the 1970s. A petrol station kept the link with the old times until, in 1996, it was moved to create more parking space for customers of the supermarket.

The Larches

Towards the end of the 1930s, popular Point to Point races drew big crowds to the Larches to watch and to bet on the Tote. When Mr. Patullo came to live at Norstead Manor, he introduced races across the fields, towards Pratts Bottom. The Larches is a house, built in 1820 and listed in the Appraisal Area Report of Bromley Borough, the name also being in general use for the whole site surrounding the building itself. It has had a varied existence, being used for many purposes. In its early days two oast houses and a malt kiln were on the Larches site. They no doubt made use of the hops, which were grown up on the hillside as far as Holly Road. There was also a well at The Larches.

In 1906 another owner, Mr. Adolphus Cohen, built an indoor rifle range and a Rifle Club held competitions there for the National Rifle Association.

The Larches present day. G.R.

The Larches house was, in common with The Elms and The Poplars, used during the heyday of Fox's Brewery as a residence for some of the brewery's senior staff. During the First World War, when the troops of the Shiny Seventh's were using the brewery building as a barracks, some of the officers were housed rather more comfortably at The Larches.

During the 1930s the grounds were used to house Botton's Fair, for Carnivals and Fetes and one Bank Holiday Fair was marred by the death of a young boy in a tragic accident. *(Orpington & Kentish Times 7.8.31)*

Later, in the 1940s, a riding stable flourished at The Larches, which was run by W. Searles (Royal Artillery). 'Ride and keep fit' was the motto and 'Well mannered Hunters' were offered for sale or hire, with tuition at '7/6d. (38p) if with Experienced Masters' or 'Hacking at 5/-(25p)' per hour.

The Larches is currently used for the sale of caravans and the Orpington Caravan Centre has kept the attractive old house in good order.

The Depression

Times were not always prosperous, however, for at the end of the 1920s came the depression and some of the social activities ceased, perhaps for lack of support, perhaps because of financial hardship.

In June 1932 the Grand Sale and Fete at Chelsfield Church was obviously a great disappointment for, after much effort, the sum raised was only £36.9s.7¹/2d. (£36.48) and the Rector's comment in the magazine was 'People just don't have the money, that's the long and short of it. We suffer from the prevailing depression'. Advertisements for items for sale in the magazine, such as 'Nearly new dark coach built pram' offered 'on easy terms', ran for several months without tempting buyers.

The effect of the depression was very obvious at the local Union Workhouse at Locks Bottom, part of Farnborough Hospital. The unemployed were means tested and given benefit for a time but when the 'dole' ran out for an individual he was given 'outdoor relief' in return for manual labour at the Workhouse Unemployment Yard or on some local site, organised by the Workhouse authorities. One local project completed in this way was the levelling of the Glentrammon Recreation Ground, with its dugouts and trenches from World War One. In 1933 these were filled in by unemployed men from 'the Yard at Locks Bottom' *(Orpington and Kentish Times 17.2.33)*. In 1934 this outdoor relief was taken over by the Unemployment Assistance Board.

Toc H

Times of depression can lead to an awareness of community needs and in 1932 a local branch of Toc H was formed by Messrs. G.R. and A. Rickard and Mr. P. Pilbeam, the Headmaster of Green Street Green Primary School. The Toc H organisation had been formed during World War One by a group of young men seeking to better the social conditions of their fellow men, by establishing clubs and hostels.

The local branch first formed a cricket club and then a boys club. There were thirteen members of the branch with a large following in only six months. Apart from running the two clubs, service to the community was the aim, through fund raising for charity, gardening, hospital visiting, organising concerts, whist drives and distributing Christmas gifts to the needy etc.

During the years 1939-1945 Toc H's war effort involved many schemes, including the collection of salvage, entertaining local Civil Defence workers and Land Army girls serving locally and organising parcels of comforts for the Forces overseas.

Towards the end of the war it was the Toc H branch which instigated the Model Village Plan about which mention is made later. It also, largely through Mr. Ivan Taylor, secured from Telcon the use of the old coach house premises, which became the village Community Centre.

Toc H was to continue with many postwar activities, helping to run the Community Centre until the mid 1970s, starting an Over-60s Club, and running the Sports at the Farnborough and Orpington Fetes for many years. From 1965-1979/80 Toc H joined with the Green Street Green Scout Group to run the annual Village Fete on the Common.

Toc H still meets in the Greenwood Centre and still serves the community, helping various causes with practical assistance, such as driving for the Orpington Club for the Blind, as well as by fund raising. Much has changed since the Thirties but there are still needs in the community and it is still the aim of the members of Toc H to try to provide for those needs.

World War II

1939 to 1945 formed a watershed in history and brought tremendous changes in the lives of individuals and the community as a whole, including the village.

Green Street Green like all Kent felt the impact of the war most severely during the aerial warfare of the Battle of Britain in 1940 and 1941. Much time was spent in air raid shelters, although it was tempting to ignore safety

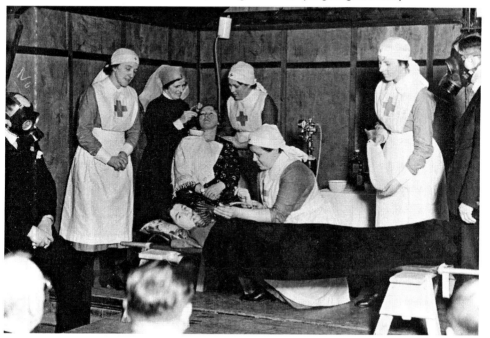

A practice Casualty Station at St. Mary's. (Orpington Times 1938)

and watch the aerial dog fights. The village had the protection of balloon barrage sites in the field at the end of the 'Tree Roads' and at The Highway. The RAF men lived in tents on the field next to the old brewery. Villagers were asked to offer them the use of bathrooms etc.

There were shelters at Vine Road School on a grass bank, where the new building stands and the cellars of the old brewery building also provided protection. In recent years air raid shelters were found during the building of Wardens Field Close sheltered housing, when a ventilation shaft was uncovered. The naming of the Close provides a reminder of that time and is a memorial to the Civil Defence personnel of the area, who had their air raid post on the corner of the field. When the siren sounded, a van would rush through the village from Locks Bottom police station to sound the siren at Pratts Bottom.

The proximity of Biggin Hill airfield meant a great deal of activity overhead, as R.A.F. planes attacked enemy planes trying to destroy the airfield. Normal life was often disrupted but sometimes the people of Green Street Green decided on business as usual. In the 'History of St. Mary's Parish Church' Miss M. Love described how rehearsals for plays took place when 'Guns all around were raining down shrapnel on to the tin roof'. In September 1940 All Souls Church, Pratts Bottom, could not be used for a few weeks because of damage from a land mine which fell nearby. It was a long bombardment for the people of the area, for when the Battle of Britain was over there were still the weapons of surprise attack to come. The V1 flying bombs and the V2 rockets, which gave little or no warning, made the final stages of the war as hazardous as when air attack had been at its height. Indeed the last V2 of the war fell in Orpington as late as March 27th 1945.

The Model Village

Although peace did not come until 1945, already in 1943 people's thoughts were turning to 'after the war'. Judging by the plans put forward in October 1943 by members of Toc H and others, there can have been few other communities where the local people had hopes greater or sights set higher for the future of their community, than in Green Street Green. At an open meeting that month a copy of the 'People's Plan for Green Street Green' was put forward and adopted by the 'Green Street Green Model Village Association'. A copy was lodged with the Town-Planning Sub Committee of Orpington Council. The authors of the scheme were Mr. J. E. Brittenden of Glentrammon Road, Mr. H. H.Bull of The Spinney and Mr. C. J. Burnett of Homestead Road, all local men with 'considerable experience in architecture, surveying and town-planning'. *(Kentish Times 5.5.44)* Had this scheme borne fruit, we would indeed have had a 'model village' of grandiose proportions. A Sports Centre, with facilities for cricket, tennis etc. including two pavilions, would have occupied an extended recreation ground between Windsor

Drive and the anticipated orbital roadway. It was proposed that this would serve the whole Orpington area. A village hall, clinic and library, a secondary school and nursery school were all planned to enhance the village. New housing would be kept within bounds to preserve the compact shape of the village and avoid unattractive ribbon development. It would also maintain the spirit of a village community. A coaching centre and 'civic restaurant' completed this ambitious design.

Green Street Green would be the envy of the world, the authors believed. Indeed copies of the plan were requested from and sent to many places, including all parts of the U.K, forces depots in Italy and Egypt and to the Government of Australia Planning Dept., all similarly looking forward to peacetime. The failure of this Utopian scheme to materialise was probably inevitable in a post war period of austerity and shortages, for the cost in money and the disruption to people would have been enormous. The previous piecemeal development of the village would have been swept away by the planners' dream of a new town with everything neat and orderly. To many people it is that very mixed development of Green Street Green, which gives the village its character. A community which, like Topsy, 'just growed' is maybe a more interesting place in which to live than a dream town. Mr. Brittenden was remembered in 1953 in the building and naming of the housing in Brittenden Close and the shops in Brittenden Parade.

Brittenden Close. (Bromley Libraries O10/50)

The Green Street Green Association

Although its plans were never implemented, the Association thus formed continued. It joined with the Beechwood Residents Association in 1948 in deciding that a Community Centre was needed for the village and Telcon was approached concerning the letting of the old Coach House in the High Street. Telcon generously granted the lease at a peppercorn rent of one-shilling (5p) per annum. It needed much work to provide it with the facilities for a Community Centre and so fund raising was set in motion. It went on from 1949 to 1951, when at last enough money had been raised for the Greenwood Centre, as it was to be called, to be opened in 1952. The Centre was then available for use for social events for all age groups of the community. The 'Model Village Association' became known from then on as the Green Street Green Association.

Thirty years later the freehold of the building became available from Telcon and the Association worked hard, (once again successfully) to raise the necessary funds which, with some assistance from the Council, made possible the outright purchase of the Centre.

Fund raising was the order of the day once again when, during the great gale of October 1987, a tree crashing through its roof extensively damaged the Greenwood Centre. It was a considerable achievement to raise the £8,500 necessary to supplement the insurance money plus a grant from the Council.

The Greenwood Centre present day. (Bromley Libraries 010/30)

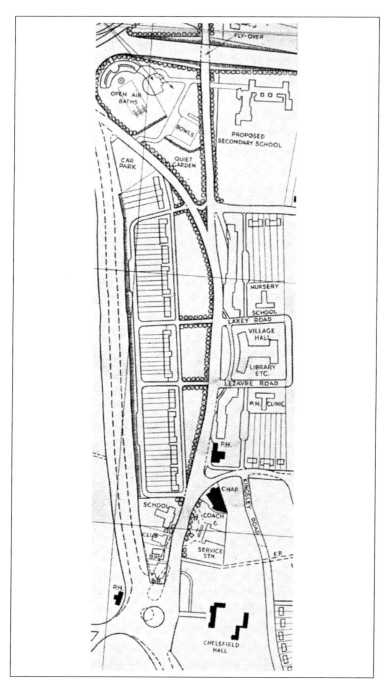

Plan for the Model Village (Orpington Times 1944).

The Centre, better equipped than before, thrived again and there is an impressive list of organisations which use it on a regular basis; the Greenwood Camera Club, Over 60s, Women's Institute, Green Street Green Flower Arrangement Group, West Kent Wine Club, Dog Training classes, Yoga class, Greenwood Nursery School, Toc.H and of course the Green Street Green Residents Association itself all bear witness to the many people who, since 1948, have supported the need for a village community centre.

To celebrate the millennium an imposing clock was installed outside, facing the High Street and the extension to the inside further improved the facilities available for those using the centre in the 21st century.

The Great Storm

On the night of the great storm in October 1987 considerable damage was suffered in the village, not only to the roof of the Community Centre. Some of the large old trees were lost from the High Street, blocking the road, damaging fences and demolishing the bus shelter opposite the Queen's Head, whilst at Pratts Bottom a fallen tree caused some damage to the roof of All Souls Church. Many houses and other buildings had structural damage to roofs, walls and windows.

The following morning was reminiscent of wartime mornings after a night of air raids, as people emerged to view the damage and compare notes about

The Great Storm 1987. M.K.

experiences. With all roads blocked and no buses or trains running, commuters had an enforced holiday. The school was closed, as were the service stations and the supermarket. Lack of electricity meant that neither petrol pumps nor cash tills could operate.

There was plenty of work, however, as neighbours helped each other to clear trees and other debris and to do emergency repairs, until such time as the roofers, builders, glaziers etc. could cope with the enormous work load which stretched for months ahead.
Many people swapped storm stories, often humorous. When a garden shed left one garden during the night and appeared in a neighbouring one next morning, it elicited the tongue-in-cheek challenge, "Have you got planning permission for that shed?"

The local postmaster was due to move house that day to South Wales but, with no petrol available and roads blocked, his departure was delayed, people commenting that he couldn't bear to leave the people of Green Street Green. Owners of open fireplaces cast covetous eyes on the fallen tree trunks in anticipation of the log fires to come but were frustrated in their designs by their non-functioning chain saws. A day later when the electricity was restored the air was alive with the whine of such saws from all directions. Meanwhile the owners of gas ovens and hobs were supplying hot drinks and food to electrically starved neighbours. It was a time of great community spirit in Green Street Green.

The power supply was restored locally within 36 hours but the clearing up of fallen trees and the repairing of roofs, fences etc. went on much longer. Some roads, notably Old Hill, were out of use for some weeks.

A Local Denehole

People in different parts of Kent will be familiar with chalk pits or 'deneholes', dug in the past perhaps to provide a dressing to improve the soil. Some of them may have been subsequently used as storehouses or have become covered up or forgotten. However, few people will have had the introduction to them that befell the residents of a comparatively new house in World's End Lane, who in May 1987 were alarmed to find that a large hole had appeared outside the front of their house overnight. It proved to be a denehole and was satisfactorily filled in and the house was made safe after their frightening experience.

Shops and Shopkeepers

In the 1960s the village shops in the High Street and World's End Lane reflected the life style of generations of village people, who had shopped for

Waitrose Supermarket present day. G.R.

their basic needs daily or two or three times a week, normal practice in the days without fridges, freezers and cars. Nowadays the weekly (or even monthly) shopping expedition has become common. Whether the advent of the supermarkets created the change or simply catered for it is a chicken and egg debate but having a supermarket in Green Street Green changed the village High Street radically. In 1977 the John Lewis Partnership chose the old coach site near Brittenden Parade for a Waitrose Supermarket as there was felt to be a gap in the market at the southern end of Orpington. When on February 28th 1978 the store was opened, although there was some resentment at the effect on small shops and at the invasion by shoppers from further afield, the new supermarket quickly became popularly accepted. Now we also have a variety of other shops, of which few come into the category of 'village shop' in the old sense. A few decades back there were three greengrocers, two grocers, two butchers, a fishmonger, a chandler and a draper, all supplying the more basic needs of the local people. They have largely been replaced by premises offering useful services whilst the Waitrose supermarket caters for most of the everyday requirements. However, there is still a butcher and a baker in the row of shops, originally known as 'The Broadway', which was built in the early years of the twentieth century between the present school field and Lezayre Road and which included both corners of that road.

The butcher's shop in The Broadway has kept its usage throughout the years for it was a butchers as far back as 1912, when there was a local sensation caused by the butcher, Albert Geere, attempting to commit suicide by cutting his throat. The shopkeeper next door, Robert Appleby, was alarmed at the sight and called the doctor and the police, whereupon Mr. Geere was taken to Cray Valley Hospital. Happily he recovered.

Arthur Wales, son of the baker, in the 1940s. E.A.S.

The bakers' shop next to the Post Office was originally a manufacturing bakery, which has changed hands several times. In the early thirties it was run by the Shepherd Brothers, described as Bakers and Pastrycooks. Then, Mr. E. J. Wales, a disabled veteran of the First World War, owned it and in addition to baking would cook Christmas turkeys for customers in the large ovens. In the late 1940s, it was sold to Stanley Woods who remained until the company's bankruptcy in 1985. Since then the shop has been part of the Plaxtol Village Bakery chain.

The Off-Licence shop on the corner of Lezayre Road was at one time occupied by one of the familial names of Green Street Green, when Mr. A.Crafter had his shop selling clothes, boots and shoes. Originally coming from Deptford, the Crafter name occurs repeatedly in many connections in Green Street Green. In 1838 Peter Crafter was a tenant of a cottage and garden at Simons Haw (World's End Lane) owned by Sir George Farrant. He was aged 41 and had five children and a servant, so was presumably a widower. By 1871 he had moved to live with his daughter, Ann Gregory, in a cottage in the High Street. At this time James Crafter, aged 30, was listed in the census returns as having a shoe shop. He was later described as a

The shops of Mr. Geere and Mr. Appleby 1912. B.M.

draper. It was probably his son, Arthur, (aged two in 1881), who was the Arthur Crafter who ran the shop selling clothes, boots and shoes on the corner of Lezayre Road in about 1912.

In 1871 William Crafter, aged 54, was described as a maltster living near the school and probably employed by Fox's Brewery. He was apparently a successful man for he owned the old cottages on the corner of World's End Lane. He let some of them and allowed one of them to be used as a meeting place for the local Baptists. He died in 1883, after which the site was bought by Mr. Morrison, also a maltster with Fox's, for a permanent chapel site.

One of the James Crafters built a house at the foot of Old Hill. He made gates from his garden on to the Common land, for which he was rebuked and ordered to lock them. He disputed the order, citing a similar infringement by the Fox family at Beechwood but this was declared to be a footpath from 'time immemorial' and James Crafter had to comply, though under protest. (Farnborough Common Minute Book December 1896).

A century later the Common land on Old Hill was still a source of dispute. James' voice had also been raised in January 1896 at Chelsfield Parish Council over the taking of gravel and flints from a gravel pit at Pratts Bottom.

The Crafter family was responsible for the early building in Laxey and Lezayre Roads. In recent years the family still had a connection with the area, one of the Countryside Wardens for the Nature Conservation Service of Bromley Borough at High Elms being another Peter Crafter.

Next to the Baptist Chapel site stood a real 'village shop' until the late 1950s. The building was there as early as 1875/80 or even earlier and it was certainly a shop by 1900. Later for very many years Mr. G. E. Hancock ran it, as a newsagent and tobacconist selling confectionery and stationery. It was yet another place where 'Teas' were advertised.

Until 1926, at the rear of this shop and Roffeys next door, (with its petrol pump), were some old timbered cottages with thatched roofs. In the census returns of the 19th century, these were recorded as being occupied by labourers with large families and by widows caring for orphans of the parish. There are several references in the 1871 census to a 'nurse child' living with a widow, this being a way for the Parish to discharge its duty of looking after orphans.

The old weatherboard building in front of the site of the former Social Club belies its age, for it has been there for over a hundred years, probably since 1870 or so. It was once a village store and had its moment of glory in 1937,

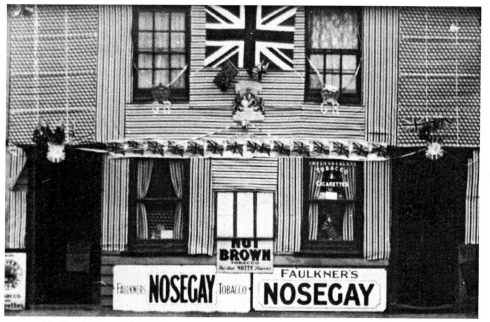

Mrs. Stead's shop in 1937. B.M.

when it was highly decorated with silver paper from tea chests to celebrate the coronation of King George VI. The proprietor, Mrs. Stead, won the prize for the best decoration in the village. She was at that time selling stamps, sweets and tobacco. It continued to be a sweet shop and tobacconist in the days of Mrs.Tullett, who also ran a lending library. The alterations and additions when Mr. Print took it over made it look good for another

'Mr. Print', 1991. B.M.

GEORGE H. MORRIS,

Licensed to let

Open and Closed Carriages,
Waggonettes, etc.

On Hire by the Hour, Day or Job, on the most
reasonable terms.

Orders by Post and Telegram punctually attended to

☞ TRAINS MET AT ANY STATION.
BY APPOINTMENT.

Work done with Horse, Cart and Van.

Postal Address:

ELM ROAD, Green=Street=Green.

Advertisement from the Chelsfield Parish Magazine, 1917.

hundred years but Mr. Print has now moved to premises a couple of doors away in a former antiques shop.

The village Post Office is now on the corner of Lezayre Road in one of the old 'Broadway' shops. An earlier Post Office was up in World's Lane on the corner of Ash Road until the end of the 1960s but the first one was in the High Street opposite the present petrol station. Henry Mussell was the Postmaster in 1878, running the shop as a general store in the end house of the row of Brewery houses. Thomas Mussell took over from 1896 until 1915. It is now a Betting Shop.

High Street Shops, Green Street Green present day. G.R.

Not all businesses were run from the High Street. In 1917 George H. Morris of Elm Road advertised as follows in the Chelsfield Parish magazine, his 'Work done with Horse, Cart and Van'. Then in 1930, G. Morrice, also of Elm Road, advertised his business in the St. Mary's magazine as 'Furniture Removers and Cartage'. It was not just coincidence that the names sounded the same. The second spelling had appeared in a census way back in 1871 when William Morrice, an agricultural labourer, lived with his family somewhere near the bottom of Cudham Lane or Old Hill but somehow the spelling was changed to Morris. Not until many years later, when checking a birth certificate at Somerset House, was the mistake discovered and the family reverted to the original spelling. The haulage removal business operated with horse drawn carts and vans and, by the early 1930s, competition from motor vehicles proved too much for survival. In 1935 it was Wells and Tomlinson who were advertising their motorised haulage and removal business from Anchor Villa, Elm Road.

The small row of shops at the beginning of World's End Lane did include a butcher's and the fishmonger's until the 1960s but has changed hands a number of times to cater for services (plumbing and hotels abroad) and Chinese food and 'Cakecraft'.

The changes in the High Street shops and businesses reflect the alterations in society that have taken place in the life of the village over the years, particularly in the second half of the twentieth century. Two newsagents are perhaps the nearest to the old 'general' shops of yesteryear. Laundry and ironing shops offer services for all, not just the Fox family and Glentrammon Garden Centre (now closed) took the place of the old Hillcrest Nursery. An indication of a more affluent lifestyle is in two hairdresser's, a barber's and an estate agent's, while there are shops and offices dealing in interior design, health & beauty, and chiropractic. Safes, locks, fishing tackle, insurance, accountancy, building plans and domestic services are on offer in other premises. Green Street Green is now a prosperous semi-urban village.

MESSRS. FOX & SONS. OAK BREWERY. FARNBOROUGH. KENT.—NEW FERMENTING HOUSE

Oak Brewery in its hey-day about 1900. B.M.

CHAPTER 5

The Brewery

Home brewing had been a long established practice on most farms and in many cottages and the consumption of beer had been for many not simply a pleasurable indulgence but a reward for labour. The Farnborough Vestry accounts have frequent entries of amounts expended on beer for the workers whose wages were low. For example: -
'1762 Pd. for beer when ye poor house was thatch'd . 4s. 6d.' (22¹/2p)
'1771 Pd. for beer at several times. 4s. 8d.' (23p)
It was also consumed during the meetings themselves, as indicated by the entry for the October 1717 Vestry Meeting: -
'Pd. for two pots of porter . One shilling.' (5p)

Hops were grown locally on the slopes of the valley up World's End Lane and near the Larches. Samuel Woodhams lived at Oak House and, in the old malthouse built in 1708, he brewed what was apparently considered the best ale in the district, using the pure water from a well nearby. Samuel and his wife Mary were people of some standing in the community and were residents of the parish of Farnborough (then still part of Chelsfield) for about sixty years.

Samuel had been brewing successfully for some time. In 1808 he leased to Frederick William Taylor premises including a malt house and malt kiln and he was paid £650 as goodwill not to pursue brewing in opposition to Taylor. The fourteen-year lease was to be determinable optionally at seven or eleven years. In 1815 Woodhams had apparently thought better of this agreement for he gave Taylor notice to quit, presumably in order to resume his own brewing. Taylor contested the notice and local arbitrators were called in to decide the matter. They failed to agree and the dispute was referred to Thomas Fuller of Farningham to act as umpire. He ruled that Taylor could retain the lease until 1818. *(Kent Archives)*

That year Taylor leased land from George Norman between Cudham Lane and 'Tonbridge High Road', (presumably the road to Pratts Bottom) and Samuel Woodhams was able to begin a brewing business again.

It was at this point (1818) that he asked his niece Susannah and her husband, John Fox, who lived at Hatfield, to come to live at Green Street Green and take over Oak Farm. The move was to be significant not just for the family but for the village, for when Samuel died in 1825 he left the farm to Susannah and her husband and when three years later she died it was bequeathed to her husband and sons. Their enterprise was to stimulate the need for housing, for education for the children and for facilities for social activities and religious meetings.

Oak Brewery was founded in 1836 and it prospered under the management of John and his sons, John Woodhams and Thomas Samuel. The family took their position in society seriously, providing over the years houses for the senior employees, cottages for the workers, a school for their children and a club room-cum-chapel for their leisure time. They were following Samuel Woodhams' lead in this for he had been for many years a Farnborough Parish Overseer, attending to the needs of the poor of the Parish and in his will he had left £20 for that purpose.

Inside a shed at the brewery about 1900. B.M.

The Brewery employed building maintenance men, carpenters, blacksmiths, wheelwrights, coopers etc. so that the firm could rightly boast of its self-sufficiency. The stable accommodation and care of the horses was a model for employers of the time and in the later years of the Brewery each May 1st. Mr. and Mrs. St. John Fox judged the gaily-decorated brewery drays parading before the daily round. Mrs. Fox presented prizes for the best decorated horse and man.

As the business passed to John Fox's sons and grandsons the Brewery became more widely known, winning awards for the ales and stouts it produced. The family continued to play a big part in local affairs as local landowners and benefactors. Their interest in the village school in the High

A decorated dray about 1900. B.M.

Street was not solely in its management. Members of the family, including Mrs. John Woodhams Fox were often involved in the daily activities of singing, reading and particularly in the girls' handicrafts of knitting and sewing. The family home moved from Oak House to the house called Beechwood in about 1880.

Despite the success of Fox's Ales (a special brew for King Edward VII's coronation met with some acclaim) the family's financial affairs were not well managed and in 1909 considerable debts forced the closure of Oak Brewery. To the hundred or so workers this must have come as a great shock, for John Fox's two Grandsons were such prominent local figures both as school managers and in St. Giles Church, Farnborough. Thomas Hamilton Fox was also a Justice of the Peace. How what had been a flourishing firm for some seventy years could cease to exist must have seemed incredible. Oak Brewery including its buildings, equipment, horses and public houses etc. all went for auction and the workers became unemployed. The debts were paid off by the proceeds of the sale although the building itself did not sell at the time. The workers must have had to seek work further afield for there was no other large employer in the village.

Not only had employment been lost but also the established social life was threatened. The Fox family had started a social club for the brewery workers where games were played and concerts held, talented local people performing songs, sketches, recitals and recitations. It is recorded in the Chelsfield Parish magazine in 1906 that 'Green Street Green Village Club had travelled by brake to West Wickham to compete in billiards, draughts, dominoes, whist and cribbage'. They scored fifteen points against West Wickham's fourteen and in those pre-radio and television days this occasion must have been a highlight. There was a quoits team, too, which in 1908 took part in the Bromley Quoits League. The clubroom was also used, by permission of Mr. Fox, prior to the building in 1905 of St. Mary's Church, for Sunday evening church services and Mothers' meetings.

Fortunately the Village Club did continue after the closure of the brewery and was open to anyone over the age of sixteen if approved by the committee, of which Thomas Hamilton Fox Esq. J. P. was the President. The rules make interesting reading by today's standards. They forbid the sale, consumption, or presence of intoxicating liquor on the premises, ban betting or gambling and order that 'Any person using bad language shall be fined 1d. for each offence'. Quaint though these rules seem now, the Club was undoubtedly then a most important feature of the village.

The Social Club was rebuilt after a fire in 1936 and Mr. P. Pilbeam, Headmaster of Vine Road School, a member of the club for 25 years, re-opened it officially in October 1936. It was a popular place for recreation for the rest of the century until it closed in 2001.

In the hey-day of the Brewery its cricket team spent many hours on the ground, now occupied by Brittenden Close, where famous players such as H. G. D. Leveson-Gower (Captain of Surrey), A. E. Relph (of Sussex and England) and others appeared. Many leisure hours were spent here, the Oak Brewery Cricket team playing against village teams from the surrounding area. In 1894 the Oak Brewery team was complimented in the Chelsfield Magazine on playing 'only bona-fide members' compared with other teams who played 'outsiders' when having difficulty in mustering a strong team. The compliment is followed, sadly, by 'but we doubt if they will maintain the system after the whopping they had to put up with at Goddington'. Team rivalries were obviously intense. Before John Fox made this cricket field available, Chelsfield or Goddington had been the local cricket venues. With the demise of the Brewery such organised social events were lost to the unemployed workers. Maybe the performances of the St. Mary's Cricket team today are re-kindling the cricketing heritage of Green Street Green, which developed at this period.

After the Auction of the Brewery a Sevenoaks brewery bought the private trade, goodwill and retail licence and for a time used the old Brewery as a store.

The two Fox brothers kept connections with the village, particularly with Vine Road School, until their deaths, Thomas Hamilton in 1923 and Walter St. John Fox in 1929. St. Giles Church has the family grave and several of the church windows are testimony to the Fox family as local benefactors.

The premises served a very different non-commercial use a few years later as a barracks during World War One. At various times the Seventh London Regiment (known to the local people as the 'Shiny Sevenths'), the Welsh Guards and the Thirteenth, Fifteenth and Seventeenth London Regiments were billeted in Green Street Green, the men in the Brewery buildings and the Officers at the Larches.

The brewery as a barracks, WWI. B.M. (Library 010/07)

One resident, Mrs. Doris I'Anson, recalled hearing as a child, 'Come to the cookhouse' being sounded and seeing the soldiers lining up at the bottom of Laxey Road with their mugs and plates to collect their meals. She remembered, too, her aunt earning a bit of extra money by washing the shirts of the Army Officers.

The men were kept in training up the hill at Glentrammon Recreation Ground, where dugout trenches were made for instructing the troops in field engineering and bombing and also at the 'Dump', which was used as a rifle range. The Dump at the back of the Green was subsequently used for many years as a site for burying refuse and now houses gritting salt for the roads in winter.

In an attempt to relieve the monotony for the soldiers the local school and churches organised some social occasions, the Baptists placing their Sunday school room at the disposal of the men for recreation on weekday evenings. The school band of the Orpington Orphanage entertained the men at the

Sports day, WWI. (Bromley Libraries O10/18)

The brewery in the snow 1916. (Bromley Libraries O10/37)

barracks and played to those who were setting off from the station at Orpington on their way to France. Football matches were played on the former brewery cricket ground, which lay between the barracks and Oak Farm. A sports day was also organised for the troops. Because of the large number of men involved it was not possible to accommodate them in local churches for Sunday services so their Church Parades were held in the open air, about where Brittenden Close is now.

At the beginning of November 1918 the Poplar and Stepney Rifles moved into the barracks and it was their band therefore which was able to celebrate the Armistice of November 11th by entertaining a crowd of patients from Orpington Hospital, gathered in the main road of the hospital. When eventually the troops moved out they were granted the privilege of a ceremonial march through the High Street with fixed bayonets - a stirring sight for the local people who regarded them as part of the community.

After its occupation by the troops during World War One the building was largely unused for many years. Brief attempts to use the site first by the Kent Mushroom Company and then by a tile manufacturer came to nothing and parts of the site began to be unsafe.

This ode was published in the Orpington Journal in March 1932 about the main chimney on the site: -
"Brewery shares are booming but there's nothing doing here
And even the brewery chimney is looking slightly queer.

Felling the brewery chimney, 1937. B.M.

Instead of brewing Chelsfield Stout it seems inclined to lean
As if it's tired of Farnborough and yearns for Green St.Green.
The highbrows say it's just as safe as if it stood up straight
And all that's happened is it's had a few---one over the eight."
In 1937 the leaning chimney of Green Street Green was felled, a spectacular
event for the local people with the traffic being stopped one Saturday
afternoon for an hour, while the Catford firm of Spears brought the
structure down. Much of the building was demolished too, with the
exception of the underground vaults.

In 1938 the site was cleared for sale and development and in 1940 the firm
of Telegraph, Construction and Manufacture, (later 'Telcon') moved in as its
premises in Greenwich were felt to be at risk. The firm manufactured high
frequency cables for vital communications and needed safe storage space for
a dispersal factory. The vaults of the old brewery building provided just such
a place. By the end of the war manufacturing of cables was taking place in
what was then called 'The Frequency Works'. Whilst some of the workforce
transferred from the Greenwich premises there was also employment for
local people both during and after the war. A couple of shops opposite were
used to make aircraft parts. There were complaints from local people that
a by-product of the use of gutta percha in the manufacture was the
disagreeable smell, which pervaded the district.

The site continued in industrial use by Telcon Plastics and its successor
Medway Packaging until 1992 when it was offered for sale. In 1994 plans
were made for the village to grow even more significantly when the

Medway Packaging, 1990. G.R.

subsequent building proposals aroused a storm of protest. When it was known that a large superstore was envisaged, local residents opposed it vigorously, on the grounds of traffic congestion and the adverse effect of a second superstore on the character of the village. Despite various amendments to the scheme by the developers, planning permission was refused and housing plans were passed instead, which was the preferred option of many of the local people.

The Oaks Estate, 1998. G.R.

Woolwich Homes developed the site with attractive three and four bedroom houses, setting out, with roads and landscaping, a compact estate named "The Oaks" between the A21 and Green Street Green High Street. The character of the site has thus become residential once again after about one hundred and fifty years of industry. Frequency Cottage, where Fox's coachman used to live, and the Greenwood Centre which was the coach house are still there but now nothing else remains of Oak Brewery.

Reminders of the beneficence of the Fox family do still remain in the existence of the old School building and the two rows of four and three stone-built houses, which were erected in 1867 for workers at the Brewery. In their day, with their out houses at the back, they were perhaps the height of luxury in what was still a rural area. The first house in the row of four was the Post Office from about 1878 until the 1930s.

The other legacy left is that Green Street Green has three public houses. At one time there were in fact four, perhaps to be expected in a village with a

Longfield, 1955. B.M.

brewery. Until 1972 on the corner of the Brewery site next to Warden's Field Close stood the house called Longfield. This was formerly 'The Poplars', John Fox's first public house which was later used as a residence for one of his senior employees.

At the other end of the High Street stands the round-ended building, which was the original Royal Oak, now occupied by the Bombay Brasserie. From 1870 to 1881 Robert Arrow was the landlord of what was then called the Fox and Grapes, later renamed the Royal Oak. This inn was part of what has been known to local people as the 'Round house' or 'Middle house.' As recently as 1990 a sign was uncovered, painted in gold and black on the rounded end wall, declaring it to be the premises of the original Old Royal Oak. The word 'Bakery' was also visible but all traces have now been painted over.

In 1930 the Royal Oak moved next to the school to occupy the site of 'Arkies', once a brewery house, 'The Elms'. Much later in 1982 it was completely rebuilt as a mock oast house for the Beefeater chain of public houses and restaurants. Meanwhile the 'Middle House' was occupied by a variety of businesses at different times, Cafe, Bakery, Doctor's Surgery and Nautical Equipment Suppliers, now the Indian restaurant, Bombay Brasserie.

Across the A21 from the Royal Oak is the more traditional looking Rose and Crown public house. Exactly when the first inn was established at the

The Royal Oak present day. G.R.

bottom of Old Hill is unclear. 1672 is one date but 1787 is a more likely alternative. It was a convenient stopping place on the London to Rye and Hastings road to rest horses before or after negotiating the steep hill to Farnborough. Very likely there was an alehouse there from the days of regular carriers using the road in the late seventeenth century but perhaps the later date of 1787 refers to the existence of an inn actually named the "Rose and Crown".

In the nineteenth century it was quite a large hostelry, for the census returns of both 1841 and 1871 show a number of people in residence in addition to the Innkeeper and his family. Some of those named were of independent means.

The early inn stood forward of the present site and there were other dwellings alongside. With the Green and pond in front it was a popular halt for travellers, from the days of coaches through to horse buses and motor buses.

It was also the meeting point for the cyclists who converged on Green Street Green, whilst in the early years of the twentieth century it was a vantage point to see officers of the Royal Artillery from Woolwich taking part in a drag hunt to Knockholt. This would have been an exciting occasion for the local people. The old coach house tradition is perpetuated (after a short gap) by the use of the forecourt as a terminus for local buses.

Motor Bus outside the Rose and Crown, 1920s. A.R.

The hunt in front of the Rose and Crown, early 20th century. B.B.

The modern Rose and Crown. G.R.

THE POND. GREEN-STREET-GREEN.

The pond in front of the Rose and Crown, 1920s. A.R.

The position of the Rose and Crown did have one disadvantage, so the story goes, for customers who imbibed too freely were wont to leave the inn and suffer a soaking in the pond outside if they were a little unsteady on their legs. In 1895 it is recorded in the Farnborough Common Minute Book that Robert Arrow wanted to rail in the pond at Green Street Green and later fill it in and build upon it. The Board refused him permission and threatened legal action if he should proceed. Some posts were erected but his neighbours removed them. Unfortunately the Minute Book does not explain why Mr. Arrow wished to remove the pond, though if he were the Robert Arrow who had been a local innkeeper, perhaps he was sympathetic to the plight of unsteady customers. The pond was eventually filled in during the 1920s, though in heavy rain there is frequently flooding in the road by the roundabout in front of the Rose and Crown. Attempts have been made to cure the problem, so far without complete success.

The Queen's Head, early 20th century. J.B.

During the years of prosperity, Fox's Brewery owned the Rose and Crown and Fox's Ales were sold there. When the Brewery closed in 1909 the inn, together with two cottages, was sold for £4,100. It was taken over by a firm called Noakes. When the Green Street Green and Farnborough by-pass (Farnborough Way) was planned the Rose and Crown was unfortunately in the line of the road. The old inn was demolished in 1927 and the new one built further back. The old houses next door also went and the people were re-housed in the newly built Coachway Cottages, which are behind on Old Hill. The village green was converted into a roundabout on the A21.

The Queen's Head, present day, (Bromley Libraries)

The third present day public house, The Queens Head, stands opposite the Social Club, set back from the corner where it stood in the early nineteenth century. On a map dated 1769 on the corner of World's End Lane (then a mule track leading up towards Chelsfield Church) a building is marked which was perhaps the forerunner of the present Queen's Head. The inn certainly had its name by 1807 when someone called Baruch Wood was described as 'Under tenant of the Queen's Head'. The late Victorian building (1899) remained a village pub until 1994 when, after complete refurbishment, it became one of the 'Big Steak' chain of pub/restaurants. Recently, in the year 2000 it once again underwent a major change, with structural changes to the outside and a complete overhaul inside by Ember Inns. Something of the appearance of the Victorian building remains amongst all the changes, so that a link with the past has not been lost completely.

There was evidently no rivalry between the public houses in the 1930s, for there was a tragic event involving the wives of the three publicans. They were in an accident while driving to the races at Brighton and, sadly, the wives from the Queens Head and from the Royal Oak were killed. The people of the village must have felt a great sense of shock and sympathy for the publicans.

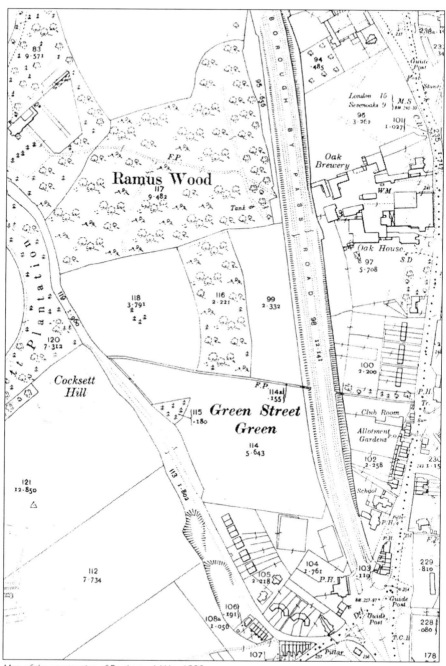

Map of the construction of Farnborough Way, 1920s.

CHAPTER 6

Transport and communications

The Hastings road via Bromley, Sevenoaks, Tonbridge and therefore via Green Street Green and Pratts Bottom became, in the nineteenth century, a busy thoroughfare from London to the coast for both travellers and goods.

Coal Posts

One commodity passing by road into London through Green Street Green was coal and duty had to be paid by the merchants transporting it. Duties were also charged on wine. Collection points were established all around the Metropolitan area. The money collected was used for public works, from the rebuilding of London, including St. Paul's, after the Great Fire of 1666, to the construction of Holborn Viaduct and the welfare of City of London orphans.

A Coal Post. G.R.

In 1861, over two hundred metal posts were positioned encircling London to mark the collection points. One stands at the bottom of Old Hill and another near the junction of the High Street and Farnborough Hill.

After the London County Council was set up in 1889, the collection of coal dues was abolished. However, the Victorian coal posts have been kept as historical landmarks, notwithstanding the remarks, in 1906, that Green Street Green has 'an extraordinary number of old City of London cast iron posts indicating the boundaries of the old Coal and Wine due area. It seems as though the

City, having delimited those bounds in a fifteen miles radius from London and come at last, full circle, to Green Street Green found itself with a surplus stock of posts and so set them up here, rather than be at the trouble of taking them home again.' *(Harper p.5)*

New roads and traffic hazards

Diversions to the old coach roads to find more convenient routes necessitated, as traffic increased in the nineteenth century, cutting across old country lanes and ancient mule tracks. It is also recorded that 'Hop gardens, fruit plantations, gorse bushes, woods, fields, meadows, fir plantations, orchards, gardens etc. were all cut through'. *(Warlow p.42)*. This comment was made when the Turnpike Act of 1835 allowed the making of the New Road from the Rose & Crown, Dunton Green to Pratts Bottom Gate. The local landowners, among whom were numbered Alderman Atkins of Halstead Place, George Polhill and Thomas Waring of Hewitts (an ancestor of Arthur Thomas Waring who wrote a 'History of Chelsfield' in 1912) did not like the changes and felt resentful. Over a century later, local people in the 1950s felt similarly apprehensive when the London Ring road threatened to cut through Green Street Green.

Coaches ceased the long haul up Rushmore Hill when the new road was made from Pratts Bottom. The old Bull's Head Inn was able to have the door above its main door bricked up, as can be seen today, when it was no

The Bull's Head at Pratts Bottom present day. G.R.

longer needed for loading luggage on to the tops of coaches. A diversion was also made from the New Inn at Farnborough to Green Street Green when, in the late 1850s, using the labour of returned Crimean War veterans, Farnborough Hill was given a hard surface. The last tolls at Pratts Bottom were collected in about 1865, 'it is said at 1/2d. (25p) per wheel'. (Judith Hook). The tollhouse was demolished in 1927 for road widening, with the foundations being uncovered and removed in 1945 when sewers were laid. The direction post which stood near the toll house pointed four ways, one up Rushmore Hill to Knockholt, one to Sevenoaks, one to Chelsfield and the fourth, not to London or even Bromley as one might expect, but to the Workhouse (at Locks Bottom). Perhaps this was an indication of the likely priorities of a traveller on the road in the 19th century.

Road accidents are not the invention of the twentieth century as the account of a journey in 1841 confirms. *(Harper p.55)* In that year the Hastings Mail met with disaster just after passing the tollgate. 'It was going about 8 M.P.H. when it ran over an old woman seated in the middle of the road, helplessly drunk. In some marvellous way the coach passed over her without doing her any injury except a slight bruise on the forehead. The passengers and guard got down nervously, expecting to see a shocking sight, but were instead assailed by a vigorous torrent of abuse.' Two miles further on the coach was in collision with a string of wagons coming from Tonbridge and the coachman died from his injuries.

Earlier than this report, the Farnborough Registers of Burials include the following: -
'1804. A poor lad, James..........found dead in the street by a Wagon running over him - per Coroner's Inquest Decr.28.'
'1806. Dodson a poor Woman who was killed by a wagon passing over her body as she was coming to pick hops, aged 63.'
It seems incredible that people could not have avoided the few vehicles there were in those days, noisy and relatively slow moving, as they must have been.

As many as nine coaches a day in 1839 left the George and Dragon at Farnborough for London, presumably most of them having come through from Tunbridge Wells. Twenty-seven wagons per week passed through Green Street Green on the way to Tunbridge Wells and Hastings in 1838. The brewers' drays from Fox's Brewery also contributed to the traffic locally. As the Brewery flourished the number of horse-drawn drays increased, until there were twenty-eight regular weekly deliveries being sent to many places in the South London area.

Legislation was later introduced to make lights on vehicles compulsory at night. Not all areas enforced this rule at first but Surrey Council led the way. One of Fox's draymen, driving through Croydon one night without lights was caught and fined heavily. His pleading ignorance of the law was not accepted as an excuse. Brewery traffic for the Oak Brewery was not the only traffic connected with the industry, for each autumn the hop crops of Kent were conveyed by road to London and the road through Green Street Green was one of the routes used. Long lines of pair horse wagons lined up for a rest by the way in front of the Rose and Crown.

The area became a pleasure ground for day-trippers from London, especially on the Bank Holiday in the summer after it was established by an Act of Parliament in 1871 by the owner of High Elms, Sir John Lubbock.

Pratts Bottom was situated at a convenient distance for a day out in the country, picnicking etc., as an account by the painter James Ward tells. He writes of leaving behind the slums of London to spend the day at 'a public house between two hills, the green with willow trees, sheep, geese, fowls, the farriers and wheelwrights at work and the gate near the overhanging wood'. This description related to before 1800 but was probably still valid throughout much of the nineteenth century.

The green in front of the Rose and Crown at Green Street Green became a great gathering point for people, pony traps and horse-drawn carriages with tearooms flourishing in the village. The employees of Bryant and Mays Matchworks chose it as their venue for their four-in-hand outings. Small wonder that, with so much horse-drawn traffic, there was a smithy alongside the green by the Rose and Crown. The smithy continued into the twentieth century at the rear of 'Middle House'. It was run by the Bidewell family (Henry, then son Frank) from 1914 and it continued to co-exist with the up and coming motor trade a few years later when Henry Junior opened a

The Smithy early 1920s. B.B.

garage selling petrol, while his wife ran a tea shop called The Cyclist's Rest. In 1960 the smithy closed and became a workshop for the garage, then run by Henry's grandsons, Cyril and Doug. They moved in 1967 and their successors concentrate on the sale of motor tyres.

Central Garage, with Harry Bidewell, 1950s. B.B.

The Railway

After the railway reached Orpington (1868) and Chelsfield (1876) both began to be commuter dormitories. There was a plan in 1894 to extend the railway line from Bromley and Hayes to Farnborough and thence eventually to Green Street Green. According to the Bromley Record this proposal was greeted with a mixture of feelings. 'Large property owners will see visions of compensations and ground rents. The working classes will anticipate an increased demand for labour, both skilled and unskilled, while shopkeepers hope to share in the good times, which a brisk labour market invariably brings. The quiet retired resident will alone be left in the cold. He will see no advantages but rather a dreadful prospect of invasion of the charming country lanes by the savage hordes of South Londoners in increased numbers.' Perhaps such a resident had memories of the effect on the area of the thirty or forty thousand attending race meetings at the High Elms course along Shire Lane some thirty years before.

The Bicycle

The popularity of the bicycle turned Green Street Green into a Mecca for cyclists, with the green in front of the Rose and Crown being a favourite meeting place and the various tea-rooms doing a brisk trade, particularly at weekends in the summer. The village remained, for decades, a centre for cyclists, with its specialist cycle shop in the High Street.

The shop belonged to H. R. Daws for many years and then in more recent times it became Ken Bird's Bicycle Centre, until it closed as the twentieth

Cyclists outside the Rose and Crown, ealy 20th century. B.M.

Advertisement from 'The Orpington Journal' 1936.

century closed. The tradition was revived briefly in 2002/3 when part of the premises of the former Glentrammon Garden Centre became a cycle shop called 'Cycle Shack'. The future of the whole site now looks uncertain.

At the roundabout, which replaced the green when the A21 was built, one can often still see in the summer lines of competitive cyclists racing through to destinations further afield, their lightweight cycles so different from the cumbersome machines of a hundred years ago. It was small wonder that they then chose to stop at Green Street Green, for refreshment at the tearooms, after the hilly ride from South London.

Even less comfortable would be the ride on a 'penny-farthing' bicycle like the one that used to be displayed, for many years, outside the cycle shop. It is hard to believe that one could reach much of a speed on such a machine. There is, however, a story of an inhabitant of Green Street Green mounted on a penny-farthing being chased by a policeman on horseback one Saturday night, from the old gravel pit to World's End Lane, for some unknown misdemeanour. Whether he was apprehended is unknown but it is a far cry from police car sirens and helicopter searchlights.

In 1972 Green Street Green had its own flourishing bicycle club for youngsters, founded and run by Brian Loakes. The tradition of cycling for pleasure was maintained for some twenty years with at one time a membership of 500. *(The Story of the Green Street Green Cycling Club, by Philip D. Turner)*

The 47 bus outside the Rose and Crown, 1930s. B.M.

Buses

By the end of the nineteenth century stagecoaches had had their day, being superseded by the railways. Local traffic was by horse drawn buses. In 1905 these horse-drawn vehicles, too, began to disappear when the first petrol driven buses were used in London. The solid tyre models of the 1914 period were finally withdrawn from Bromley Garage in October 1933. *(Blake p.74)*

Transport facilities had improved by the 1930s when the London Passenger Transport Board had three omnibus services passing through Green Street Green and there were two Green Line coach services. Penfolds ran a coach company for private hire and they were well patronised as few families had their own cars.

The mixture of horse-drawn and mechanical vehicles led to what would now seem bizarre incidents, for example the case of the drunken Deptford costermonger in 1934. *(Blake p.111)* He drove a pony and trap down Farnborough Hill on Bank Holiday Monday, following a zigzag course and overtaking not only other ponies and traps but motor cars too. He was pursued by a police patrol car and was subsequently fined £1 for being drunk in charge of a pony and trap.

Roffreys about 1930. J.B.

The new motorised vehicles needed fuel and an early petrol station in the High Street was J. A. Roffey's, situated where the present Total Service Station stands. A pump outside dispensed petrol straight into cars waiting in the roadway. Earlier, the establishment had advertised Pratts Motor Spirit and Vacuum Motor Oils, catering largely for motor cycles.

For many years a horse trough stood as a local landmark on the corner near to the inn sign of the Queens Head. Then, as reported in the Orpington and Kentish Times in October 1936, it was queried as to whether there were enough horses to need a trough, since the corner really required widening. The age of the horse drawn vehicle had come to an end, though it perhaps returned briefly during the wartime petrol shortages.

Road developments

After World War Two a London ring road was planned which would have had a major effect on the village. Land was left undeveloped pending the building of the road between Warren Road and Windsor Drive. Much of the Common would have been destroyed and this Outer London Orbital Road would have dominated Green Street Green. The construction, instead, of the M25 gave the village a reprieve for which almost everyone must have been grateful. The resulting increase in traffic on the A21, though marked, cannot compare with what it might have been. More recent new road layouts and roundabouts have improved the traffic flow and safety for the village.

Bus services are perhaps almost as frequent as some thirty years ago when fewer families had cars but now local services have been tailored to the needs of residential areas since the deregulation of the bus companies in 1988. The Roundabout buses, now First Bus, operate in roads never previously served by public transport. The old Green Line route through London to Windsor has gone but other bus services to Bromley and elsewhere provide links for journeys further afield. Metrobus has recently increased the frequency of the service through Green Street Green because it is so well used.

Metrobus (now part of the Go Ahead group) has, since 1983, had its depot on the site of the Fox family's Oak Farm, along with some car repair works. The Botton family, fairground people who lived at Green Street Green from 1935 until the 1960s, once occupied the site. Their rides and amusements were based there, when they were not on the road touring Kent as a travelling fair or operating on the field in Cudham Lane next to The Larches. One of the brothers invented an amusement machine known as the Cascade. To the right of the main entrance stood, until demolished in 2003, two houses built by the Bottons and named appropriately, 'Fairground' and 'Roundabout'.

When old Mr. Botton died in 1938 his funeral was a big event in the district. His days as a horse dealer were commemorated in the wreaths shaped as horse collars and one in the form of a pony from his grandchildren.

Metrobus Depot, present day, (Bromley Libraries)

The funeral of Mr. Botton, 1038. B.M.

During the time of the Bottons, space at Oak Farm was rented out, as it is today, to a number of other small businesses, chiefly in the motor trade. There were tentative plans in the 1980s for a different commercial development of the site but Metrobus now seems firmly established.

Traffic problems, part of modern life, will continue to be of concern in Green Street Green but improvements have been achieved by local pressure groups such as the Green Street Green Residents' Association, most notably the mini-roundabout at the junction of the High Street with Farnborough

Hill and Glentrammon Road. The Association remains vigilant on all local issues, particularly concerning parking and housing development.

Yellow lines and parking restrictions are also a feature of the High Street and some roads leading from it. Huge lorries need to negotiate the entrance to

By-pass under construction. P.L. 1920s.

An A.A. patrol man on duty, early 20th century. A.R.

Waitrose and despite the parking limits there is still often congestion. Ours is not the only village High Street to suffer from this modern affliction and at least it is spared some of the through traffic which speeds past along the Orpington and Farnborough By-passes.

It is a long time since the A.A. man stood outside his box opposite the supermarket site with no traffic to supervise other than two parked bicycles by the deserted green. The A.A. man has now been replaced by visiting traffic wardens checking for illegal parking.

CHAPTER 7

Religion

The first Green Street Green churches

Until the Twentieth Century the Anglican parishioners of Green Street Green and Pratts Bottom had to attend services at either St. Martin of Tours at Chelsfield or St. Giles the Abbot in Farnborough, both churches being in the endowment of the Manor of Chelsfield. They had the same incumbent until 1876 when St. Giles' first had a separate Rector. Worship involved

All Souls Church, Pratts Bottom present day. G.R.

travelling on roads and tracks, often badly affected by extremes of weather. As the population increased, around the end of the 19th Century, there was a need for local buildings for worship and All Souls Church was built at Pratts Bottom in 1890.

In Green Street Green the Club Room (on the site of the later Social Club), built by the Fox family for the employees of the Brewery, was used for a service every Sunday evening and for Mothers' Meetings. Sunday School services were held in the School Room.

In 1898 the new Rector of Chelsfield, the Rev. J. J. Baddeley, conscious of the size of the Parish, felt that a site for a Mission Church in Green Street Green should be secured and a new parish should be formed. It should consist of Pratts Bottom, Green Street Green and part of Farnborough Parish on the main road through Green Street Green.

The first St. Mary's Church. Green Street Green about 1920. A.R.

Inside the first St. Mary's Church, Green Street Green about 1920. B.M.

In 1900 the Parish Magazine drew attention to the problem: - 'One portion of the Parish of Chelsfield is increasing considerably through building operations. 'The Green' as it has been called, will not be so much longer, as the beautiful sloping meadow is cut up and marked out by the Agents for the erection of villas and, although within two miles of the Parish Church, it is hardly to be expected that the future inhabitants of 'The Green' will find their way so far for worship.'

A. C. Norman Esq. of The Rookery, Bromley Common, met the need for a church with a gift of land in Worlds End Lane and in November 1905 the Rector, under licence from the Bishop of Rochester opened a Mission Church. It cost £300 and about £250 was raised before the opening, the Archbishop of Canterbury donating two guineas. The building was regarded as temporary and so, by 1908, money was already being raised for a permanent church. Again, in 1910, Mr. Norman gave land for this purpose with provision for a vicarage. The temporary building was named St. Mary's Church and served as a place of worship for over thirty years, during which many kinds of fund raising events took place.

The Norman family, the benefactors of St. Mary's, were landowners of some substance, owning property in Belgravia as well as in the Bromley area. Chelsfield Hall Farm had been in the family since 1807 and is still today owned by them through the Rookery Investment Company. Members of the family lived in Chelsfield, taking an active part in the social life of the church and village there in the early years of the twentieth century.

The Parish of
St. Mary's Green Street Green

The upkeep of the Mission Church, the purchase of a house at Hillcrest Nursery for a parsonage and the enlargement of the Church Hall (1928) all required funds.

Thanks to some generous grants from Church organizations, Mrs. A. C. Norman, widow of the donor of the land, laid the foundation stone of the permanent church at Green Street Green in July 1937. The Bishop, in the presence of some three hundred people, consecrated the building on a foggy day in November of that year and in 1938 (Aug.5th.) the new Parish of St. Mary's, Green Street Green was constituted. The Rev. W.T .H. Sampson who had been Curate in Charge became the first vicar. All Souls' Church, Pratts Bottom, ceased to be a Chapel at Ease to St. Martin's and became part of the Parish of St. Mary's.

The outbreak of war interrupted many church activities, particularly outdoor events, but during these years a number of religious dramas were staged at St. Mary's, rehearsals taking place despite shrapnel raining down on the hall's tin roof. All Souls' Church, Pratts Bottom was damaged by enemy action in 1940 and could not be used for services for a few weeks.

St. Mary's Chrurch present day. G.R.

Green Street Green Baptists Church present day. G.R.

The Parish grew rapidly after the War. In 1955 the house called St. Leonards, opposite St. Mary's Church, built on the site of Simons Haw, was purchased by the Diocesan Authorities to replace the parsonage, which was sold. The 'Hall and Church Extension Fund' covered the cost in 1960 of a new Church Hall, Lady Chapel and Vestries.

Thirty years later the development continued and further facilities were provided through additional buildings to mark the Jubilee of St. Mary's. These included Sunday School classrooms and a lounge and enlarged kitchen, enabling the Parish Church to make a greater social and pastoral contribution to the community in Green Street Green.

The debt that the community owes today to those who gave their lives in the two world wars was recognised, by the dedicating of an additional memorial for those who died in World War One. They had not previously been listed on the memorial in the church building. In the year 2000 a Garden of Remembrance was created in the Church grounds for parishioners to commemorate their departed loved ones.

The Baptist Church

Local Baptists had originally met in one of the old cottages, on the corner of World's End Lane and the High Street, owned by Mr. William Crafter, one of the Brewery employees. Then Mr. Ebenezer Morrison, (another Brewery employee) had bought the corner site and meetings were held in an iron building, erected behind the cottages. In 1899 the Baptist Church of Green Street Green became independent of Orpington Baptist Church and a fund

The opening of the Baptists Church Hall, 1923. B.M.

was started to replace the iron building. In 1907 the present day church with its distinctive spire was built. The old iron building became the Sunday School room, until money was raised for a new one, which was opened in 1923 in memory of Mr. J. M. Higgs, the late Superintendent. The original iron building remained at the back of the church until the late 1980s, when it was removed.

The Methodist Church

Methodism had been followed in the area for some 150 years before the opening of the church in Windsor Drive. It would not be unreasonable to surmise that John Wesley himself (1703 - 1791) perhaps visited or at least passed through Green Street Green and Chelsfield, as he made his way on horseback to the church at Shoreham. He was welcomed there as a preacher because the Vicar, the Rev. Vincent Perronet was a friend. Small groups of Wesley's followers gathered in rural areas and we have evidence of one such group, from the windowpane of the kitchen at Hewitts, on which was scratched, 'A Methodist Meeting established at Chelsfield 16 of February 1812'. This historic pane of glass may now be seen in the vestry of the present church in Windsor Drive.

The Methodist Church, Chelsfield about 1967. P.L.

It was not till 1840 that a regular place of worship was used. Under the leadership of Thomas Verrells, a room at Crosshall Cottage in Chelsfield village was rented at 1s.6d. (7^{1}/2p) a week and services were held on Sunday evenings, in wintertime by candlelight. In the room above, services were held by the 'Bible Christians' (the name deriving from the fact that they all carried Bibles). Chelsfield was put on the Sevenoaks Circuit at this time. Some thirty years later the generosity of Mr. Thomas Townsend, who purchased a plot of land nearby, made possible a permanent chapel.

After the Second World War there was a growth of population in the Chelsfield Station area and a Sunday School was started in Warren Road. In 1959, monthly services were held in Windsor Drive in a Nissen Hut, which was used as a Community Centre and by 1960 all the evening services were held there. Then, in 1964, Council land next door, which had been originally earmarked for a filling station, was bought for the sum of £3000, following a petition by Mrs. Nancy Adams. The old chapel in Chelsfield village was sold and the foundation stone of the present church was laid in November 1966. The building opened in May 1967. In 1971 the church became part of the Orpington Circuit and 1992 marked its Silver Jubilee.

The Free Church

At Pratts Bottom in the early years of the twentieth century non-conformists held meetings in each other's front rooms until, in 1928, the Congregational Church was built further up Rushmore Hill from All Souls Church. It was named the Free Church, United Reformation. In 1998 that church became part of the Ecumenical Partnership in Pratts Bottom together with All Souls Church, under the new Associate Vicar of Green Street Green Parish.

The Roman Catholic Church

No Roman Catholic Church has ever existed within the Green Street Green Parish boundary. The nearest place of worship, for people in the village of the Roman Catholic faith, is Holy Innocents Church, on Strickland Way off Sevenoaks Road. In 1979/80 a new church was built to replace the original building, which had been in use since 1909.

The Brethren

A community, fairly new to Green Street Green, meets in a building set back from the road by the roundabout on the A21. It is now the Meeting House of the Brethren, many of whom live locally and who have met in the Farnborough area since before the First World War. *(Blandford p.7)*

The site itself has had a chequered history; having previously housed a fitness club, a Judo club and having been originally one of Green Street Green's many cafes. It was known as the 'Pavilion' and dances were held there during World War Two.

CHAPTER 8

Education

The first schools

In the early years of the Nineteenth Century village schools were few and far between in Kent. Indeed 'by 1830 not more than a dozen Kentish villages possessed elementary schools '(Jessup p.140). More than a hundred further schools were to be opened by 1860. Among those was one in Green Street Green in 1851.

A school had been built in Chelsfield in 1823, supported by subscriptions in addition to fees. This was demolished in 1864 when the present school was built, on the same site, from voluntary contributions. Meanwhile John Fox's brewing enterprise in Green Street Green had proved successful. He provided homes in the village for his employees and, in 1851, the school in the High Street for their children. The school flourished and whereas prior to 1851 children had to go to Chelsfield or Farnborough for schooling, now some children from other villages came to Green Street Green. Members of the Fox family even taught occasionally at the school.

Soon after the passing of the 1870 Education Act, Green Street Green School, assisted by Government grants, became a Board School and in 1876 schooling became compulsory for children aged five to thirteen years. A school was built at Farnborough, which helped to relieve the pressure on school places at Green Street Green. The Farnborough School Board, elected by local ratepayers, had the Fox family represented on it and controlled both schools. Similar schools were set up in Chelsfield in 1884 and in 1886 at Pratts Bottom. Mr. Charles Pearson was Head for 21 years, from 1883, with his wife teaching the youngest class.

In rural areas school attendance conflicted with the desire to supplement the family income, through child labour in the home or, for example, in the fields fruit picking. Much encouragement was given to children to attend regularly and the Chelsfield Church Magazine reported names of children at Chelsfield and Pratts Bottom who had not been absent or late, on the principle that regular attendance leads to proficiency - and a bigger Government Grant. There was also the incentive of prizes. In Green Street Green by the turn of the twentieth century, the school in the High Street was overcrowded and understaffed. At one time two classrooms had to accommodate well over one hundred children. Up to thirty older pupils had to walk to Pratts Bottom each day in order to make room for the younger ones.

A new school is needed

The overcrowding at Green Street Green was the result of house building, largely on the Chelsfield side of the High Street. It led to children attending school at Chelsfield or Farnborough and calls for a new building in Green Street Green. This caused arguments locally because Green Street Green was divided between the Parishes of Chelsfield and Farnborough. The school in the High Street had associations with the Fox family and Farnborough, whereas the increase in the child population was on the other side of the High Street. Mr. Fox was quoted in a report in the St. Mary Cray and Orpington District Times on 15th September 1905, as saying, in a letter explaining that he could not attend the enquiry, that there were no grounds for enlarging the present school. He also said that neither he nor his brother intended selling any land for this purpose, unless they were compelled to do so. 'As the houses are on the new side of Green Street Green it appears to me that's where the school should also be, where there is plenty of land for building a school for the older children, leaving the old school for the infants and younger children. I have always held this view and see no reason for altering it now.' At the meeting, a spokesman for the Farnborough Parish stated that they had enough school room for their own and seventy children of Chelsfield, whom they had been educating for some years. So if the ratepayers of Chelsfield required a school they must pay for it.

In 1909 the new school in Vine Road was opened officially by Lord Avebury and the occasion was celebrated at a Tea Party. This building (3 rooms and a cloakroom) was to house the older children--up to the age of thirteen (a few were a little older) whilst the old building was to become the Infant School. The new school was the responsibility of the Chelsfield Parish Council and the Infant School was under Farnborough. Each had a separate Head Teacher.

Following these changes there was a welcome period of stability with the appointment of Mr. Percy Pilbeam as Headmaster of the upper school, for he was to hold the post and live in the School House on the High Street for 30 years. Although there was flexibility on the exact age of transfer from the Infant School to the school in Vine Road, the number of pupils was always outstripping the number of places. Further classrooms were added at Vine Road in 1933/4 before some relief came with the opening, in 1936, of Central Schools in Charterhouse Road, Orpington, (to which children over the age of eleven were moved) and then of Warren Road Primary School in 1938.

Mr. Pilbeam and his class in the 1930s. B.M.

Wartime school

In 1939 there were many problems for the Local Education Authority. The Infant School in the High Street was closed and some of the children went to the Junior School. Though reopened in 1942 for normal education, it was to be interrupted again in 1944 by air raids including 'flying bombs'. The dangerous situation led to the evacuation of pupils and a reduction of the rolls by the end of the war. The Junior School 'soldiered on' with unavoidable interruptions due to enemy activity in the air. Much time was spent in the air raid shelters but every effort was made to offer as normal an education as possible in the circumstances.

A local hero

Meanwhile a former pupil was achieving great wartime distinction. Tom Durrant was born in Kingsley Road and attended the school in Vine Road until 1932. After leaving school he had several jobs until he joined the army in 1937, enlisting in the Royal Engineers. From all accounts he made an excellent soldier, both in the matter of military skills and in his qualities of leadership. When the Commando force was formed in 1941 Tom was amongst its strength and he was one of those selected for the raid on St.

Tom Durrant V.C., WW2. R.E.D.

The Durrant brothers, WW2. R.E.D.

Nazaire in 1942. The raid largely achieved its objective but with a heavy price in prisoners taken. One of them was Sergeant Tom Durrant, severely wounded during the confrontation between his small launch and the German destroyer, Jaguar. He died of his wounds soon after reaching hospital. His bravery in continuing the action, even while the launch was sinking, won the admiration of not only his own comrades but of the German captain of the destroyer. It was his account, which led in 1945, to Sergeant Durrant being given the highest award for valour, the Victoria Cross. At Green Street Green School in 1949 a commemorative plaque was unveiled in his honour by Major-General F. S. G. Piggott C. B., D.S.O. in the presence of his widowed mother and many local dignitaries. Durrant Way off Farnborough Hill, is named after him or, perhaps one should say, in honour of the family because his elder brother, Jack, was also a war hero, having been awarded the Military Medal for bravery in 1940 when the liner Lancastria was sunk, coincidentally near to St. Nazaire.

1944 Education Act and after

The schools serving Green Street Green were affected by the national changes brought about by the 1944 Act. At the end of the primary stage the pupils were required to sit the 11+ Examination to determine to what form of secondary education they were most suited - Grammar, Technical or Modern.

Both buildings in the village continued to be used for primary classes and in 1952 the two schools were amalgamated. Accommodation was all too often a problem as the school roll rose, in spite of the fact that the primary schools at Warren Road and the Highway provided additional places. Extra classrooms including 'Mobile Units' improved the situation. Most pupils moved on to Charterhouse Road Schools which were designated Modern Schools, whilst some gained places at Grammar or Technical Schools.

More recently most secondary schools became 'Comprehensive', although Bromley retained two selective schools in the Orpington area. New schools in the Darrick Wood and Ramsden areas were built, while the Charterhouse Road Schools were closed in 1985. The choice of available secondary schools widened, coinciding with greater mobility within and between the London boroughs, although most parents prefer to choose, given the opportunity, a secondary school near to home.

The schools in the area were not denominational, as in some parishes, but towards the end of the 19th.century the Presentation Brothers built a home for destitute and orphaned boys on a Sevenoaks Road site. From this beginning came St. Joseph's and St. Anne's Schools to which Roman Catholic parents could send their children. The primary school is still there but St. John Rigby School, West Wickham, is now the Roman Catholic secondary school for the area.

In recent years the primary Schools at Warren Road and Pratts Bottom have enlarged, with buildings and extensions reflecting the growing school population.

In Green Street Green in 1984 it was decided to close the old school building in the High Street and in 1991 new buildings were erected at Vine Road, with further extension for Resources in 1995 and 1997. Many of the problems which beset the school in accommodation and communication between two sites etc. have been overcome. The introduction of changes contained in the 1988 Education Act and the enhanced status of Governors mean that the local community is even more closely linked with the village school and its future development.

From the original village school in the High Street the old school bell was

Green Street Green School in the 1990s. G.R.

taken to the modern Vine Road building as a relic and the old school has
been found a new use. After serving the young people of the village for a
century and a quarter it now provides a service for an older generation with
its charitable status as an 'I-Care' centre, for people recovering from a
stroke. John Fox, the school's founder, would be surprised by the change
but, one hopes, would approve its continued use in such a worthwhile cause.

The 1851 school in the High Street in its present day use. G.R.

CONCLUSION

Green Street Green has grown from a tiny hamlet at the beginning of the nineteenth century to a large semi-suburban village at the beginning of the twenty-first century.

For one hundred and fifty years it had an industrial site at its heart. Now, apart from shops, offices, a few car repair works and the Metrobus depot, it is a residential village and likely to remain so if the Green Belt policy is maintained.

Where the old Shire Lane ends is the 'not unbeautiful Green' recorded by Harper in 1906 as a redeeming feature of the village. It is still attractive. Here were some of the old gravel pits, frequently mentioned as a source of dispute in the Farnborough Registers and from which some prehistoric remains have been recovered. This first Green has been protected against encroachment since, to use the old phrase, 'time immemorial'.

At the other end of the High Street is the site of the old second Green which, far from being the centre of village activity as it once was, is now a hub of noise, fumes and speed. Traffic, a dominant feature of the beginning of the twenty-first century, swirls around and away from the Green, the Street and the Green.

So, we did not solve the mystery of the origin of the name World's End. Perhaps it is best that not all mysteries are solved. World's End is no longer there but the name can continue to intrigue the curious.

'A man's reach should exceed his grasp or what's a heaven for?' Robert Browning.

BIBLIOGRAPHY

Barnard A.	'Oak Brewery', in 'The Noted Breweries of Great Britain and Ireland, 4 vols 1889-91'.
Blake L.	'Before the War' A Portrait of Bromley and District. 1929-1939.
Blandford J.H.	'Farnborough and its Surroundings'. 1914.
Copus G. (1)	'The Commons at Green Street Green and Pratts Bottom'. 1955.
Copus G. (2)	'Notes on the History of World's End, Chelsfield, Kent'. 1993.
Harper C.G.	'The Hastings Road'. 1905.
Harvey D.	'Fruit Growing in Kent in the Nineteenth Century'. 1973.
Hook J.	'Pratts Bottom: an English Village'. 1972.
Horsburgh E.L.	'Bromley, Kent'. 1929.
Jessup F.W	'A History of Kent'. 1987.
Lee M.	'Calendar' 1946 [and] '365 Facts of interest in the district', [1945?].
Waring A.T.	'History of Chelsfield'. 1912.
Warlow G.H.	'History of Halstead'. 1934.
Wright C.	'Kent through the Years'. 1975.

Newspapers

Bromley Record.
Bromley Times.
Kentish Times.
South Eastern Gazette.
The Times.
Orpington Journal.
The Smallholder

Other Sources

'Book of Orpington'. (D. Cox).
'Brief History of the Baptist Church Green Street Green'. (The Church, 1949).
'History of St. Mary's Church'. (M. Love, 1987).
'Kentish Place Names'. (J.K.Wallenberg, 1931).
'A Bibliography of Orpington'. (V.Whibley, 1972).
Various notes from the Bill Morton Collection.
'Appraisal area reports for Chelsfield & Godington and Farnborough & Crofton' (L B Bromley 1981)

ACKNOWLEDGMENTS

We are indebted to the late Alex Freeman, whose urging of the U3A Local Studies members to be active in local history projects launched us into a study of Green Street Green. For the notes and photographs of the late Arthur Rickard, which gave us the material with which to start we are also indebted. We hope that both would have approved of the result.

Our grateful thanks for advice over the years also go to Geoffrey Copus, Dr. Eric Inman, Bill Morton, and Dr. Alan Tyler. Simon Finch and the staff of the Bromley Library Local Studies Department have given their much-appreciated assistance.

We thank the following for items of information: -
The Bidewell family, Mrs. J. Bruce, Andrew Fordyce, Mrs. P. Holmes, Mrs. D. I'Anson, Mr. P. Kell, Mrs. P. Knowlden, Mr. & Mrs. L. Lewis, Rev. P. Miller, Miss M. Morrice, Mrs. D. Saint (Miss Read, Author), Mr. E. A. Sims, Canon P.A. Welsby, Mrs. J.E. Wiles.

For the loan and use of photographs we thank the following:
The Bidewell brothers (BB), Mrs. J. Bruce (JB), R.E.Durrant (RED), Mike Kempton (MK), Philip Lane (PL), Stan Mortimer (SM), Bill Morton (BM), Barry Newman (BN), E. A. Sims (EAS).

Photos credited (AR) are from the collection of the late Arthur Rickard and are used by permission of the Rickard family. Extracts from the Orpington Journal are included by permission of P. J. and P. R. Hamblin. Extracts from the Orpington Times are reproduced by permisssion of Kentish Times Newspapers.

Finally, our thanks go to Dorothy Featherstone for her invaluable technical help and Promotion Design Services for their design work.

INDEX

(Illustrations in bold)

L

M

N

O

P